ISSUES THAT CONCERN YOU

Child Labor

Laurie Willis, *Book Editor*

GREENHAVEN PRESS
A part of Gale, Cengage Learning

GALE
CENGAGE Learning™

Detroit • New York • San Francisco • New Haven, Conn • Waterville, Maine • London

Elizabeth Des Chenes, *Managing Editor*

© 2012 Greenhaven Press, a part of Gale, Cengage Learning

Articles in Greenhaven Press anthologies are often edited for length to meet page requirements. In addition, original titles of these works are changed to clearly present the main thesis and to explicitly indicate the author's opinion. Every effort is made to ensure that Greenhaven Press accurately reflects the original intent of the authors. Every effort has been made to trace the owners of copyrighted material.

Cover image © Megapress/Alamy.

LIBRARY OF CONGRESS CATALOGING-IN-PUBLICATION DATA

Child labor / Laurie Willis, book editor.
 p. cm. -- (Issues that concern you)
Includes bibliographical references and index.
ISBN 978-0-7377-5690-6 (hardcover)
1. Child labor. 2. Child labor--Government policy. 3. Child labor--United States.
4. Child labor--Government policy--United States. 5. Child labor--Law and legislation--United States. I. Willis, Laurie.
 HD6231.C4513 2011
 331.3'1--dc22
                                                                        2011016582

Printed in the United States of America
1 2 3 4 5 6 7 15 14 13 12 11

CONTENTS

According to the Anti-Slavery Society, "The total number of children involved in the [carpet-making] industry in South Asia is very difficult to assess, but in India the South Asian Coalition on Child Servitude estimates that between 200,000 and 300,000 children are involved, most of them in the carpet belt of Uttar Pradesh in central India. Similar numbers may be working in Pakistan and up to 150,000 in Nepal." A 2010 report from the United States Department of Labor supports this assertion, stating that child laborers have been found in the carpet industry in five countries—India, Iran, Nepal, Pakistan, and Afghanistan.

Some children who make carpets work alongside their families. Although some people believe that child labor is always wrong, others disagree, saying that working in a family business should not be viewed in the same way as working for someone outside the family. Jacobsen Oriental Rugs explains it this way on its company website:

> Although in a completely beneficent world anyone would prefer to see children everywhere in the world have a Western-style childhood with the opportunity for a sophisticated education, we do not see child labor within the family unit as a horrible thing ("within the family unit" is the crucial phrase). Weaving learned from a mother, grandmother, father or brother is a specialized skill which can produce a cash income for the weaver and the family. If the choice is between stoop labor in the fields and weaving, there is no question but that weaving is by far the better life.

Other children are treated as bonded servants or slaves. They may be working to pay off a debt of money that their parents owe, or their parents, unable to support them, may have sold them to the carpet factory. Working conditions for these children are extremely difficult. The United States Department of Labor reports that

> in India, hand-knotted carpets are usually made in small workshops or loomsheds. Most of India's child weavers are young boys. Children may work 10 to 14 hours a day six to seven days a week. They receive little or no time off, even when sick or during holidays. The long days spent in poorly-lit and cramped positions result in injuries and work related illnesses. Cuts and wounds are common. Loom owners have been known to "treat wounds by putting sulphur from match heads into the cuts and then lighting them on fire, thereby sealing the wound." By the time many of these children reach the legal employment age, their hands are badly damaged, their eyesight has grown weak, and their growth is stunted.

One of the justifications used to explain why children are needed to work in the carpet industry is the claim that their small hands are needed to tie the knots to make quality carpets. In reality, young children are not skilled enough to make high-quality carpets. Those are made by adults, who have the knowledge and experience for this more sophisticated task. Children are used to make cheaper, low-quality carpets.

The number of children in this industry has decreased significantly since 1994, when an organization called Rugmark, now known as GoodWeave, was formed. This organization monitors the work of carpet factories and certifies that carpets sold with the Rugmark or GoodWeave label were made without child labor. When someone is shopping for a rug or carpet, they can help to stop child labor by only buying products with labels indicating they are certified by GoodWeave or another similar organization. Another way for shoppers to avoid supporting child labor is to look for medium- or high-quality carpets, which are usually made by adults instead of children.

Carpet making is just one example of an industry that makes heavy use of child labor. There are many more places throughout

Rugmark is an international organization that monitors the work of carpet factories and certifies that carpets sold with the Rugmark label were made without child labor.

the world where children can be found working long and hard hours for little or no pay. The viewpoints in this book examine some of the questions around the issue of child labor. They include perspectives on the hazards and benefits of various types of child labor, ideas about various ways child labor can be regulated to protect children's rights, and ways in which child labor is related to education.

ONE

Child Laborers Work Under Difficult Conditions

David L. Parker

David L. Parker, an occupational physician in Minneapolis, Minnesota, photographs children's working conditions and public health problems around the world and has become an acclaimed advocate of children's human rights. In this viewpoint, Parker discusses what he has learned about child labor during his travels. He says that while not all work is harmful for children, many children around the world are not able to attend school because of work, and some working children have to endure conditions that are dangerous, both physically and emotionally.

When I began photographing child labor in 1992, I had no idea how many children worked, what their working conditions were like, or how difficult it would be to document the issue. Although many factories and workplaces were open and easy to photograph, others were closed and unwelcoming. To gain entry into some factories, I presented myself as a buyer of shirts, carpets, or other products for an international corporation with only a post office box for an address.

I was surprised at what lay just beyond the surface of everyday activity. In 1993, during my first trip to Nepal, I visited dozens of carpet factories where children were hand-knotting carpets in cramped, musty rooms. After leaving Nepal, I went to Bangladesh and photographed children working waist deep in leather-tanning chemicals and scavenging plastic and cardboard amid the rotting waste in garbage dumps. . . .

[My work] documents an ongoing failure to meet children's basic needs—a goal that is clearly out of reach of their families. I have no doubt that poverty forces most working children and their families to become victims of economic exploitation. Some of these situations, such as sex trafficking, make regular news headlines. But problems such as lack of schools and lack of jobs in which parents can earn enough money to feed a small family go largely unnoticed.

The Attempt to Regulate Child Labor

Seeking to protect children from what are often deplorable working conditions, national and international communities have implemented laws and treaties to regulate child labor. Since the United Nations General Assembly adopted the Universal Declaration of Human Rights in 1948, dozens of international treaties concerning children's rights have been written.

The most encompassing of these is the UN's 1989 Convention on the Rights of the Child, which recognizes every child's right to a primary school education. The convention also requires that nations protect children from economic exploitation "and from performing any work that is likely to be . . . harmful to the child's health or physical, mental, spiritual, moral or social development."

Another important treaty, the International Labour Office's Prohibition and Immediate Action for the Elimination of the Worst Forms of Child Labor, known as Convention 182, took effect in 1999. The International Labour Office (ILO), a branch of the United Nations, brings governments, workers, and employers together to promote safer and healthier working conditions. Convention 182 defines the worst forms of work as those associated with slavery and bondage, prostitution and pornography, illicit activities such as the drug trade, and other work that "is likely to harm the health, safety, or morals of children."

Children in India carry harvested crops. It is estimated that, worldwide, nearly 320 million children under the age of sixteen work.

In spite of numerous laws and treaties, child labor remains an enormous problem, and millions of children lack access to basic education. Officially, more than 320 million children under age sixteen work worldwide, and 25 percent of children do not complete a primary school education. In addition, almost 150 million children labor in the worst forms of work as defined by the ILO.

I have sometimes found it difficult to define when work is harmful, in part because of the importance of education in all children's lives. Any job, even one that does not seem harmful, can keep a child from attending school. Education provides a basis for a child's social, economic, and cultural development as well as the foundation for a healthy life. Children whose parents—particularly their mothers—are better educated are more likely to go to school and stay in school longer than children whose parents received little or no education. Further, children with less-educated mothers are more likely to work at an earlier age than children with educated mothers.

Part of a Family Cycle

For many families, child labor is part of an intergenerational cycle of poverty, social exclusion, and lack of education. Poor families frequently lack the resources to ensure that their children go to school and stay healthy. An increased risk of illness contributes to the cycle of poverty. Young women who work and go to school or who work instead of attending school tend to have less-healthy children. A woman who has been to school for even a few years is more likely to marry later, obtain prenatal care, have a smaller family, and have healthier, better-educated children.

Another difficulty in understanding when work is harmful stems from the complexity or ambiguity of some job circumstances. For example, in 1993 and 1995 I photographed circus performers in Nepal and India. Although the children are often laughing and having fun, most are bonded laborers, a type of modern-day slave. Circus owners trick families into selling their children and then force them to work many years without pay. Neither the poor working conditions nor the slavery-like situation is obvious to a casual observer.

Other forms of work harm children in much more obvious and painful ways. In 2000, I photographed children at a rehabilitation center for young combatants in Sierra Leone. The children told stories of being drugged and forced to kill their parents or mutilate their neighbors. They also reported being shot during combat or beaten if they tried to escape from military service.

Some domestic workers are held in virtual slavery behind locked doors. Although I have photographs of children doing domestic chores—preparing food, caring for sisters and brothers, and washing clothes—only once did I gain access to a private home where children were employed. The employer did not allow me to take photographs.

Children and Employment

Global estimates of all children in employment, child laborers who are either below the minimum age or subject to dangerous conditions or forced labor, and children who do hazardous work, 2008.

	Total Children	Children in employment		Children laborers		Children in hazardous work	
	('000)	('000)	%	('000)	%	('000)	%
World	1,586,288	305,669	19.3	215,269	13.6	115,314	7.3
Boys	819,891	175,177	21.4	127,761	15.6	74,019	9.0
Girls	766,397	129,892	16.9	87,508	11.4	41,296	5.4
5–11 years	852,488	91,024	10.7	91,024	10.7	25,949	3.0
12–15 years	364,366	85,428	23.4	61,826	17.0	26,946	7.4
(5–14 years)	1,216,854	176,452	14.5	152,850	12.6	52,895	4.3
15–17 years	369,433	129,217	35.0	62,419	16.9	62,419	16.9

Taken from: International Labour Conference, Accelerating Action Against Child Labour: Global Report Under the Follow-up to the ILO Declaration on Fundamental Principles and Rights to Work, 2010, p. 9.

Pathetic Working Conditions

Overall, working conditions for most children are pathetic. Many worksites lack sanitary facilities and clean drinking water. Child workers are exposed to excessive noise, clouds of dust, and other safety hazards. They eat food they find on the street or in the garbage dump, drink water and bathe in the same pond where they wash their tools and mix mud for making bricks, and live on the street or in cardboard huts.

Because children are still developing physically and mentally, harmful substances have a greater impact on them than on older workers. Pound for pound, children breathe more air, eat more food, and drink more water than adults do. Toxic chemicals such as mercury or lead can cause brain damage and permanent disabilities.

Children work long hours with little time for rest, play, or school, and even jobs that seem relatively safe place children at risk. Street vendors may leave for work at four or five a.m. and not return home until late at night. They go long stretches without eating. They may be robbed or abused. Street children often work for unscrupulous adults who refuse to pay them, cheat them of their earnings, or sexually exploit them.

Children who work face a wide array of dangers, from rats, wild dogs, and rotting wastes in garbage dumps and choking dust in stone quarries to injuries from high-speed machinery or the harsh chemicals used to tan leather. Some children develop diseases typically associated with adults, such as arthritis or skin diseases. Most children do not wear protective equipment. Even when such equipment is provided, it does not serve children well since it is designed for adults.

I am encouraged by new data indicating that the number of working children around the world has declined over the past few years. Some nations have made strides to protect child workers from dangerous conditions, yet many others still fail to keep children safe, healthy, and educated.

TWO

Actions Regarding Child Labor Must Respect Children's Rights

International Save the Children Alliance

> The International Save the Children Alliance is a world-wide organization dedicated to defending the rights of children. This viewpoint expresses the organization's views on children who work. Save the Children does not support blanket bans on child work, nor does it support child work in all situations. Instead, the group attempts to discern whether work is harmful or helpful to the child. Reasons that children work—poverty, lack of access to good education, inequalities based on gender and other factors, and varying cultural views on the role of children—are considered, as they play a part in the nature and value of child labor. Those responsible for oversight of child labor—institutions, governments, employers, and parents—are also discussed.

The adoption of the UN Convention on the Rights of the Child (UNCRC) is fundamental to the recognition and realisation of children's rights, including the right to be free from harmful work. Since then there have been a number of important developments in the field of child work. The most significant of these has been the adoption of International Labour Organization (ILO) Convention 182 on the worst forms of child labour. Other developments include

International Save the Children Alliance, *Save the Children's Position on Children and Work*. London: International Save the Children's Alliance, 2003, pp. 1–14. Copyright © 2003 by Save the Children International. All rights reserved. Reproduced by permission.

consumer concern about children's work, an increased focus on corporate social responsibility, and recognition of the effects of macro-economic policies [those that effect the larger economy as a whole] on children. It is against this background that this position has been developed. It is the result of a year-long consultation with Save the Children staff and working boys and girls.

Fighting for Children's Rights

Save the Children fights for children's rights. As part of this goal, Save the Children seeks to ensure that girls and boys are protected against harmful work.

Our goal, our understanding of children's work and our beliefs about appropriate responses are shaped by the UN Convention on the Rights of the Child (UNCRC) and a rights-based approach to programming.

Implicit in our goal is a belief that children's work is not a uniform activity and we must recognize that, while some forms of work violate children's rights, other forms of work do not. Most forms of work have both good and bad elements, and for this reason, can be both harmful and beneficial to children's development and well-being. Therefore, we accept neither blanket bans of all child work, nor an approach which unequivocally promotes children's work. We believe that different responses are appropriate for different forms of work and for different working children.

In achieving this goal, we seek to ensure that governments, families and other 'duty-bearers' fulfil their obligations to address children's rights. We also seek to ensure that boys and girls fully and meaningfully participate in decisions which affect them. Children should be enabled to exercise their rights, and the opportunities available to them should be expanded so that work is a choice, not a necessity.

Defining Child Work

Child

A child is a girl or boy under the age of 18. This includes adolescents, who are often excluded from conceptualisations of working children. Children are the holders of rights as defined by the UNCRC. We view all children as individuals capable of being actively involved in claiming their legal entitlements.

Work

Save the Children views child work in its broader sense, as activities children undertake to contribute to their own or family economy. This means that we include time spent on home-maintenance chores, as well as on income-generating activities inside or outside the home. Thus, the unpaid agricultural work of many girls and boys on family-run farms, and the domestic tasks done by many children in their own homes, are included in this definition. Work can be full- or part-time.

Our definition of work does not exclude criminal or illicit work activities. While some believe that describing activities such as the commercial sexual exploitation of children as work can be seen to legitimise these activities, we believe that including these activities in our definitions of work has two main advantages. Firstly, defining the work activities of children as 'crimes' can lead to the exploited and abused children being treated like criminals, rather than holding the exploiters and abusers of children responsible. Secondly, while we recognise the exploitative nature of these activities, the causes and some of the effects that they have are similar to other forms of work. especially other extremely harmful forms of work. This suggests possibilities for shared learning and an overlap in responses.

Harmful work

In defining harmful work, we use Article 32 of the UNCRC:

> "States Parties recognise the right of the child to be protected from economic exploitation and from performing any work that is likely to be hazardous or to interfere with the child's education, or to be harmful to the child's health or physical, mental, spiritual, moral or social development."

Implicit in this article is the belief that boys and girls only need to be protected from harmful work, and that this harmful work has a number of components, including harm to health, development and education. Distinguishing between different forms of work requires the full participation of working girls and boys.

Within the broad category of harmful work, it is also helpful to distinguish between different degrees of harmful work. In some forms of work, harm may be an inevitable part of the work, while in other forms of work it may be possible to prevent harm from taking place. Thus, three categories of work may be distinguished:

- work where the harm to the child is extreme, and where rights violations are impossible to prevent, requiring urgent removal from work. This . . . includes, among others, forced labour and prostitution.
- work where rights are violated, but where it is possible to prevent violations through improving working conditions or assisting children to find better alternatives to harmful work.
- work where rights are not violated and may contribute to the fulfillment of rights. Work which contributes to the fulfillment of rights can be encouraged.

We do not use the terms 'child labour' and 'child work' to distinguish between harmful and non-harmful forms of work, but instead use the term 'child work' to refer to all forms of child work, explicitly identifying different degrees of harm where necessary.

Children Work for Many Reasons

In this section we provide an exploration of key underlying causes of work, and of the effects of work on the realisation of children's rights, and we consider which duty-bearers are responsible for the factors that push children into work. This analysis is essential to inform our position on child work.

Poverty is often given as the key reason for children's work, and there is much evidence to suggest that many children work for their own or their family's survival. However, there is also evidence to show that some poor countries, and indeed some poor households, have been more successful in tackling harmful

Children's Views About the Effects of Work

Boys and girls identified several negative and positive effects from work.

Positive Effects

- We learn to communicate with other people
- We learn to support our families
- We regularly learn new things
- We can pay school-related expenses
- It helps me to behave with assurance and improve my speech
- We learn how to handle money
- We learn how to take on responsibility faster than other children
- We learn the reality of the street
- We get clothes and food in return for work

Negative Effects

- Can harm physical development and lead to injury
- Start liking money too much and drop out of school
- May fall under the influence of bad people
- Self-esteem can be damaged
- If we are not treated well, we suffer

Taken from: International Save the Children Alliance, Save the Children's Position on Children at Work, 2003, p. 6.

child work than others with similar resources. This suggests that, in addition to poverty, other key causes must also be explored in order to truly understand why children work.

A lack of access to good quality, relevant education is also regarded as a key reason for children's work. In many instances, boys and girls work because there are no schools for them to go to, or because the education on offer is of poor quality and irrelevant to their survival needs. The fact that education is not a viable alternative to work for many children may be partially linked to the inability of governments (because of insufficient resources) to ensure that education is genuinely free, or to invest in improvements in the quality of schooling. However, it is often a lack of *commitment* to education, and the consequent allocation of resources to other sectors, that is responsible for poor educational provision. The negative attitudes and lack of skills among teachers, and the levels of abuse in schools, are also factors that contribute to children and their families regarding work as more relevant than school.

Structural inequalities, based on gender, caste, class, religion and disability, are important determinants of both the types and amounts of work that girls and boys do. For example, children may be discriminated against on the grounds of gender, ethnicity or disability, leading to exclusion from school, limited employment prospects and little choice but to work in harmful forms of work. Gender norms can prevent women from entering paid employment, necessitating children's entry into the workforce.

Beliefs about childhood also determine children's work. While in the West, childhood is seen as a time for play and school, in many other parts of the world, work is seen to be the most appropriate place for learning and development. This can shape parental decisions about children's work, employers' beliefs about the appropriateness of recruiting children, and government legislation on child work. Working children should not always be viewed as passive victims of exploitation. Children themselves may choose to work, feeling that work offers them better opportunities than schooling, to please their parents or simply because they want to earn money.

Seemingly unrelated issues like HIV/AIDS [and] conflict and climate change can have a major impact on child work. For example, the HIV/AIDS pandemic has reduced the adult workforce and diverted expenditures away from social protection and education, pushing boys and girls into harmful work. Conflict can lead to an increase in child soldiers and to children being separated from their families, becoming vulnerable to abuse and exploitation.

Environmental disasters associated with climate change can increase household vulnerability, forcing children to work to enhance the amount or stability of incomes.

When seeking to understand children's work, it is important to remember that, for each individual working child, it is likely that choices about work have been shaped by more than one factor. For example, the primary reason for girls and boys from poor households working may be the need to earn money due to poverty. However, it may also be the case that children from poor households would continue to work even if household income were increased; if, for example, there were no schools available to provide them with an alternative to work.

Positive and Negative Effects

Work can have both positive and negative effects on the realisation of a range of child rights, and this effect will vary greatly with the type of work and with the maturity, gender and other status of the child. Younger girls and boys, and children with disabilities, may be especially vulnerable to a number of child rights violations as a result of work. Work can have a major impact on children's right to survival and development. In its worst forms, work can kill. The negative effects of work on physical development may include injuries from dangerous equipment, mines and guns, and physical abuse by employers or customers. The negative psycho-social effects of work include the psychological effects of verbal, physical or sexual abuse by employers, and feelings of low self-esteem as a result of doing low-status work. Although psycho-social impacts often receive little attention, they can be greater than the physical effects. Work can also help girls and boys achieve their rights to survival and development; for example, incomes from work can be used to pay for food and health care. Work can enhance feelings of self-esteem, through the knowledge that children are contributing to household incomes.

Work can help children to realise their right to education by paying for school fees or providing children with skills and capabilities. While some children manage successfully to combine work with education, in many cases work has a negative effect on children's schooling. In some types of work, long working hours or slavery-like conditions can mean that girls and boys are either

The United Nations Convention on the Rights of the Child has been fundamental to the recognition and promotion of children's rights, including the right to be free from dangerous work.

unable to attend school, or are too exhausted to achieve their full potential.

Work can deny boys and girls their right to protection. In some occupations—such as commercial sexual exploitation, or where children are trafficked for work—girls and boys are treated like criminals because of their work. Children may be arrested but are not always treated as minors within criminal justice systems. When children attempt to return to their communities, they may be ostracised because of the low status or criminalised nature of this work, making a return to a community/family environment difficult. Working children who live away from home while engaged in occupations such as domestic service, may also be denied their right to a family environment, and as a consequence may be deprived of protection against abuse while working.

Discrimination against working children can affect the realisation of their rights. It can, for example, lead to some groups of working children being denied access to health or education services. This may involve the discriminatory attitudes of staff against working children, or be reflected in the way services are delivered—for example, opening hours that do not allow working children to attend clinics or schools, or schools and clinics that are a long way from children's workplaces.

Work often means that children have little time, freedom or opportunity to realise their right to participate in decisions that affect their lives. However, children's roles in the economic survival of the household can also result in them taking a greater role in decision making. In some cases, children meet other children through working and join forces—through working children's organisations—to improve their rights. Working children's organisations also enable children to fulfill their right to freedom of association.

Children also have a right to leisure, recreation and participation in cultural activities. Working long hours, or having to combine work and school, may deny children this right.

Responsibility for Working Children

At the international level, key duty-bearers include the International Financial Institutions (IFIs)—such as the World Bank and International Monetary Fund—responsible for macroeconomic policies which have a major impact on the poverty that pushes many children into harmful work. Evidence shows that

THREE

New Legislation Will Help American Children Who Do Agricultural Work

Office of Lucille Roybal-Allard

Lucille Roybal-Allard is a congresswoman representing the Thirty-Fourth Congressional District. In the following viewpoint, Roybal-Allard discusses the need for legislation to change the working conditions of child agricultural laborers. She contends that the United States needs to offer protection for farmworker children. Roybal-Allard proposed the Children's Act for Responsible Employment (CARE), which would raise the labor standards for pesticide exposure, require teenagers working in agriculture to be at least sixteen years old, and serve as a stronger deterrent for employers who violate child labor laws.

Congresswoman Lucille Roybal-Allard (CA-34) introduced "The Children's Act for Responsible Employment" (CARE) today to ensure adequate protections for children working in our nation's agricultural fields.

"It is unacceptable that children who work in agriculture, one of this country's most dangerous occupations, are less protected under U.S. law than juveniles working in other occupations," Congresswoman Roybal-Allard said. "The CARE bill addresses

Office of Lucille Roybal-Allard. "Bill Introduced to Protect Farmworker Children and Keep Them in School," September 15, 2009. www.roybal-allard.house.gov. Reproduced by permission.

this inequity by raising labor standards and protections for farm-worker children to the same level set for children in occupations outside of agriculture."

Farmworker Children Deserve Protection

"Farmworker children often work long hours, use hazardous farm equipment, earn sub-minimum wages, and are continually exposed to hazardous pesticides," Congresswoman Lucille Roybal-Allard continued. "Our farmworker children deserve the same protections given to children in other industries; if they are too young they should not be working, and if they are working, they deserve protection from long hours and unsafe work practices."

While retaining current exemptions for family farms, the CARE Act (H.R. 3564) would require that teenagers be at least 16 years of age to work in agriculture and at least 18 years of age to perform particularly hazardous work. The bill retains an existing exemption that permits 14 and 15 year olds to work in certain agriculture jobs, during limited shifts and outside of school hours.

"Tragically, absent from our nation's classrooms each school year, are thousands of children who instead of going to school, will be working in the fields and orchards of our country. Studies show that an alarming 50 percent of youth who regularly perform farm work, drop out of school," Congresswoman Lucille Roybal-Allard said. "All children in our country deserve the benefits of an education. The CARE Act will help farmworker children receive valuable educational opportunities proven to be an essential pathway to a better life."

David Strauss, who is the Executive Director of the Association of Farmworker Opportunity Programs and a member of the Child Labor Coalition, said about CARE: "I commend Congresswoman Lucille Roybal-Allard for her strong effort to eliminate this unconscionable discrimination in federal law against poor, mostly Hispanic, farmworker children. I urge all Americans to contact their Members of Congress and ask them to support this important legislation."

A child gathers tobacco for curing in Virginia. US law allows children to work in agriculture at younger ages and in worse conditions than in any other industry.

Support for the CARE Act

Bruce Goldstein, Executive Director of Farmworker Justice, which is also a member of the Child Labor Coalition, said: "Labor-intensive agriculture is one of the most dangerous occupations, but our laws allow children to perform agricultural work on large

Minimum Legal Age of Children Working in Agricultural and Non-agricultural Situations

Situation

- Unlimited agricultural work with parents' consent
- Unlimited agricultural work without parents' consent
- Limited non-agricultural work without parents' consent
- Standard non-agricultural work without parents' consent
- Hazardous agricultural work
- Hazardous non-agricultural work

Age: 0   5   10   15   20

Taken from: Human Rights Watch, *Fields of Peril: Child Labor in US Agriculture*, 2010.

farms at ages when they would be prohibited from working in safer workplaces. This nation should end its history of discriminating in labor laws against farmworkers and also must substantially increase labor law enforcement in the fields. We strongly support the CARE Act."

In addition to addressing the age and hour requirements for child farmworkers, CARE addresses several other problem areas:

- To serve as a stronger deterrent for employers who violate child labor laws, the bill increases the maximum civil monetary penalties for child labor violations from $11,000 to $15,000. The bill also raises the maximum penalty to $100,000 and imposes a criminal penalty of up to 5 years imprisonment for willful or repeat violations that lead to the death or serious injury of a child worker.

- To provide children with greater protections, CARE raises the labor standards for pesticide exposure to the levels currently enforced by the EPA [Environmental Protection Agency].
- To improve information gathering, the measure requires data collection on work-related injuries, illness, and deaths of children under age 18 in agriculture, as well as an annual report by the Secretary of Labor on child labor in the U.S.

FOUR

New Legislation Will Harm American Children Who Do Agricultural Work

Darrin Youker

Darrin Youker is a journalist for the *Reading Eagle* newspaper in Reading, Pennsylvania. In this viewpoint, he discusses proposed legislation that would prevent teens between the ages of fourteen and eighteen from working on local farms. He contends that farmwork is an invaluable part of the Future Farmers of America (FFA) program, where high school students get experience working on actual farms while they are considering farming as a future career. He also says that the proposed legislation would force farmers to hire migrant workers instead of employing local teens.

A tough economy, here, among the cows, is where Devin Ruggiero comes to make some extra money. Ruggiero milks cows, cleans stalls and does farm chores at Zack Meck's farm in Marion Township [Pennsylvania] after school and during the summer. At 17 years old, Ruggiero of Bethel Township has no plans to become a farmer. He wants to be a diesel engine mechanic. But now, heading into his junior year at Tulpehocken High School, he needed a job and the farm was offering one. "They are the only place that is hiring," Ruggiero said. "It's good pay, and these are good guys to work with." Ruggiero is one of an untold number of Berks County teens who work on local farms, milking cows, baling hay and cleaning stalls. Proposed federal legislation aimed at improving the working conditions of young migrant farmers could change all that, farming organizations say. The Children's Act for Responsible Employment (HR 3564), known as the CARE Act by supporters, would have far-reaching effects on the agriculture industry, they say. Farm groups say that the legislation, as written, would prevent anyone under the age of 18 from working on a farm.

California Democratic representative Lucille Roybal-Allard proposed a measure that would prohibit children under twelve from working on farms and that would hold agriculture to the same work standards as other industries.

"That's the unintended consequence," said Ron Gaskill, senior director for congressional relations with the American Farm Bureau Federation in Washington, D.C.

Proposed Legislation

The measure, sponsored by U.S. Rep. Lucille Roybal-Allard, D-Calif., would change federal law governing young people working on farms. It would, among other things, prohibit children under 12 from working [on farms] and hold agriculture to the same standards that govern teens working in other industries.

It would make exceptions for children who work on their parents' farms.

In announcing the legislation, Roybal-Allard said she was trying to prevent the abuse of migrant farm children, who sometimes work for more than 12 hours a day for little pay.

For Pennsylvania farms, which depend heavily on labor to assist with the milking of cows, harvesting of crops and the maintaining of equipment, HR 3564 would be a decisive blow, said Mark O'Neill, a spokesman for the Pennsylvania Farm Bureau.

"We strongly oppose this legislation," he said. "The availability of farm labor is one of the major concerns that farmers deal with all the time. This defies common sense."

New Rules Would Be Burdensome

Currently, minors are allowed to work on farms, as long as they have parental consent and conditions are safe, O'Neill said.

Allowing youth to work on farms has encouraged a number of young people to pursue careers in the industry, he said.

Sheila M. Miller, Berks County's agriculture coordinator, said a number of Berks County farmers hire teenagers to assist with the day-to-day operation. The proposed legislation would be burdensome to Berks County farms, she said.

"This is where kids get real-life experience," Miller said.

Adam Serfass, an agriculture sciences teacher who supervises the FFA [Future Farmers of America] program at Conrad Weiser High School, said area farmers frequently contact him to see if

Rules For Youth Working on Farms

At ages 12 or 13...

Can be employed in nonhazardous jobs, outside school hours on farms that also employ the youth's parent(s) or with written parental consent.

At ages 14 or 15...

Can be employed in nonhazardous jobs, outside school hours.

At ages 16 or older...

Can be employed in any farm job, hazardous or not, at any time.

On small farms not covered by the Fair Labor Standards Act minimum wage requirements, youth can work in any nonhazardous job outside school hours with parental consent.

Youths of any age may work at any time in any job on a farm owned or operated by their parents or persons standing in place of their parents.

There are 11 specific hazardous occupations in agriculture that may only be performed by hired farmworkers who are at least 16 years of age. Most involve work with machinery or handling toxic or explosive materials. Some limited exemptions exist that permit 14- and 15-year-olds to perform these otherwise prohibited tasks if they are enrolled in a vocational agriculture program or have received appropriate training.

Taken from: US Dept. of Labor, www.youthrules.dol.gov.

young people are available for work. For a teen who did not grow up on the farm, the chance to work on one is invaluable, he said.

Heidelberg Township farmer David Wolfskill said he's made several calls to the FFA program in the past few years to find students willing to help with the milking. For Wolfskill, who farms more than 1,200 acres across Berks County, reliable labor is one of his greatest concerns.

It's tough to understand why agriculture is being singled-out in this federal legislation, Wolfskill said.

"Don't they understand agriculture is the backbone of this state?" he said.

Meck, who has been working in the dairy industry for 13 years, said young people in the area know to visit his farm to see if work is available. If this legislation passed, Meck said he would have to hire migrant labor.

"It's a good experience for them," he said of teens. "They learn how to work and how to manage their time."

[*Editor's note:* As of press time, HR 3564 had not become law.]

FIVE

Selling Goods on the Street Harms Children

World Vision International

> In many parts of the world, children work as street vendors, beginning at a very young age. This viewpoint starts by telling about the daily lives of children who sell flowers and fruit on the streets of Bogotá, Colombia. The viewpoint continues by explaining how legal and social work in Colombia is helping to eliminate child labor such as street vending, which the author believes harms the children. World Vision International is a Christian humanitarian organization dedicated to working with children, families, and their communities worldwide to reach their full potential by tackling the causes of poverty and injustice.

Bosa is a down-and-out neighbourhood in south Bogotá [the capital of Colombia]. Here, in the middle of Bosa's busy streets, Martha, Brandon and Aidé Paola sell flowers and fruit to help their struggling families make ends meet.

The three children are well acquainted with Bosa's darker side, characterized as it is by rampant crime, drugs and violence. Alcoholic bar patrons, aging prostitutes and aggressive strangers share the same streets where the children ply their trade with ever-present difficulties and dangers.

Martha, age 13, usually works alongside her 10-year-old sister, Aidé. Brandon, age 14, is almost always nearby. The children live in the same low-income neighbourhood about 40 minutes walking distance from Bosa. Conditions of extreme poverty compel them to return to Bosa each day.

Martha and Aidé live with their mother and eight other siblings. It was the death of their father and the loss of his income that led them to the mean streets of Bosa. Brandon's family, also large and desperately poor, has similarly come to depend on his earnings to put food on their table.

Children Purchase Cheap Goods at the Market to Sell on the Streets

The children's routine has remained unchanged since they first started working in Bosa. It starts with a long walk to the Paolquemao market in the centre of Bogotá, where they purchase the cheapest flowers, near the end of their bloom. Then they expertly clean and prune the flowers to conceal their fading beauty. Or they purchase fruit on the verge of spoiling, or maybe sweets if the flowers and fruits aren't selling well.

That done, they head to Bosa and their real work begins. Selling on the street requires patience, concentration and a thick skin when faced with hustlers and hasslers who frequent the area.

Not far away, at a busy traffic intersection, John, age 16, and Michael, age 12, are trying to sell bags of overripe fruit to drivers waiting for a green light. The pace of their work is largely dictated by traffic flow. Red lights giving them just enough time to make a hurried sale or two; green lights signalling the few seconds left to leave the intersection before passing cars reach high speeds.

John and Michael are half-brothers. Their father introduced them to their work on the streets. They do their best to steer clear of trouble and dangers that seem to wait around every corner— like the thugs and thieves who pick fights and try to rob them of their meagre earnings. By standing up to them, dodging cars, and surviving other daily rigours of their work, the boys have earned their street credentials and the respect of their peers.

The days are always long—many fruits or flowers that the children can't sell will have to be thrown or given away. Usually heading home after nightfall, the children stay on constant vigil for a potential threat. They know they can outrun most trouble if they can just see it coming. . . .

In many parts of the world, children start out as street vendors at a very young age.

A combination of factors, derived from social and economic conditions in Colombia often forces boys and girls to work in sectors that are highly exploitive and where there are risks to their physical, social and psychological development. These factors are also abetted by a system of cultural values that considers boys and girls as objects owned by their families rather than as individuals with their own rights.

The Government's Attempts to End Child Labor

It is worth mentioning at this point that the Colombian government has modified the constitution in an attempt to rectify the problem of child labour. . . .

Colombia has endorsed three "plans to prohibit and eradicate Child Labour", whose essence is to start new initiatives to prevent the early entailment of children into the labour force and to guarantee the fundamental rights of working children and adolescents, through which specific instruments will be defined to prevent and respond to this problem, including its worse forms; and to seek for alternatives so children and adolescents can enjoy their childhood, by participating in playful and recreational activities, and return to school to strengthen their human potential.

At last, Law 1098 from 2006, ratifies the Childhood and Youth Code, from October 2006, incited by government and non-government organizations (among them World Vision) who want to protect and promote the rights of children and adolescents, regarding specifically articles 20, 39 and 43 that reference the workforce minimum age and the right of protection for young employees authorized to work.

Demanding Better Treatment of Children

The visibility of child labour in Colombia constitutes a new and significant landmark, because never before had society demanded legal compliance to this type of law. Currently, the authorities find themselves obliged to fulfil their legal and constitutional responsibilities and obligations toward the children of Colombia.

Certainly, these legislative developments represent a vital change for the country and its children, but it is necessary that they become a reality in the lives of children and adolescents, through the commitment of families, civil society and State, [so that] we can eliminate this problem that deeply affects Colombia's present and future. With this objective, World Vision Colombia is engaged, working in different fronts, for the creation of more adequate laws, visibility and incidence in power circles, through the ongoing implementation of the project for the Eradication of Child Labour (ETI) in the agriculture sector.

All the initiatives previously mentioned are very important but it is undeniable that the eradication of child labour depends on the creation of better and more dignified job opportunities for parents. For that reason, prohibitive policies have to be followed with compensatory mechanisms to reduce in the short or medium term an increase of poverty. In addition, it is necessary to continue working on the cultural aspects, to guide our society to accept child labour as an educational and pedagogical issue. Although, traditionally, most Latin American cultures see this work as part of the education of children, it is absurd to maintain it as an extra-curricular activity, especially if we consider the levels of exploitation and abuse suffered by children and adolescents; low salaries, bad working conditions and extensive hours of work, as obstructions for their development.

Finally, the most worrisome consequence of child labour is the disruption to the child's physical, psychological, emotional and social development. In addition, child labour also perpetuates the poverty cycle for children that are forced, through different circumstances to work, since employment limits their access to education and knowledge, and as adults condemned to unskilled and low income jobs.

SIX

Controlling Child Labor Entails Convincing People It Is Wrong

Amelia Gentleman

In 2006, India issued an amendment to its Child Labor Prohibition and Regulation Act that strengthened the country's ban on labor for children under the age of fourteen who work in "hazardous" jobs. This viewpoint was written a year later, in 2007, when the author, Amelia Gentleman, was New Delhi, India, correspondent for the *International Herald Tribune*. Gentleman claims that the ban has not been effective, citing specific sweatshops where children as young as nine work up to sixteen hours a day making clothing. She states that a main reason child labor continues is that the people of India are not convinced that child labor needs to be reformed, so the laws are not enforced.

Tourists hoping for a glimpse of real India should ditch the well-trodden Red Fort–Taj Mahal circuit and make a pilgrimage to a little-known Moghul-era tomb hidden in the shabby residential district of Kotla, smack in the center of Delhi.

The tomb itself is in bad shape, despite the sign outside that proclaims it a nationally protected monument, but visitors are welcome to walk inside and climb up the unlit stone staircase to the roof.

This is where the excursion becomes interesting, and it is perhaps Delhi police officers, rather than tourists, who should be taking stock of the view from here.

Ugly apartment blocks have been built around the monument over the last few decades, in places barely a meter from its walls. In many of the windows opposite, young children are clearly visible, hunched over low tables, diligently embroidering sequins onto brightly colored silk and gauze.

Welcome to India's zari [sari] industry—where children labor for a pittance to stitch elaborate brocaded designs onto high-fashion evening wear for India's new rich.

Around half a dozen of these sweatshops are open to casual inspection from the tomb's roof. In the labyrinthine lanes nearby, too narrow for cars to pass through, there are dozens more.

Inside, boys as young as 9 cautiously describe their bleak working conditions. They squat on the floor for the duration of their 16-hour shifts, from 9 a.m. until 1 a.m. the following morning, for which they earn about 100 rupees, or $2.50. Food (watery vegetable curry and rice) is served in plastic buckets.

The children, all migrants from impoverished rural areas, sleep and work in the same squalid, bare rooms, their few belongings stored in plastic bags in the corner. In some places, as many as 16 live cramped together, with only a CD player to break the monotony.

This area of Delhi is well-known as a ghetto of cheap child laborers, available to do contract work for the textile industry. In the gutters outside, the raw sewage that runs down open drains sparkles with sequins. Tiny flashes of pink, yellow and green turn out, on closer inspection to be glinting plastic jewels, decorating the mounds of cow and goat dung.

Child Sweatshops Continue Despite Efforts to Stop Them

Despite repeated requests from Bachpan Bachao Andolan, an energetic nongovernment organization dedicated to eradicating child labor, and despite the presence of a police station less than one kilometer away, nothing has been done to shut down these

"APPARENTLY IT WAS MADE BY A SEVEN YEAR OLD INDIAN BOY— NOT BAD IS IT...?"

"Apparently it was made by a seven year old Indian boy—not bad is it . . ?," by Stephen Hutchinson. www.CartoonStock.com.

workshops, even though the employment of children under 14 in the zari business has been illegal for more than 20 years.

The scene broadly sums up the effectiveness of India's ban on child labor.

On [October 10, 2006,] India marked the first anniversary of the strengthening of its child labor laws. A year ago [2005], amid much media excitement and government fanfare, an amendment to the Child Labor Prohibition and Regulation Act, which prohibits the employment of children under 14 in "hazardous" jobs, was announced, extending the definition of what constitutes hazardous to include children working in homes as maids, and in hotels, restaurants and roadside cafes as low-paid waiters.

At the time, activists working in the field voiced some caution about what they felt were inadequate preparations for the rescue and rehabilitation of illegally employed children, and warned that vigorous enforcement was essential if the modified law were to be any more potent than the existing statutes.

A year [later], there is frustration at the slow pace of change.

Public Awareness of Child Labor Has Grown

On the plus side, campaigners say there has been considerable raising of awareness across the country, so that most people now realize that employing a young child as a cleaner in your home is illegal. On the less positive side, since there has been very little police action to prosecute those who continue to employ children, there is a belief that it is possible to continue as before with impunity.

"Without enforcement, awareness is meaningless," said Bhuwan Ribhu, a campaigner with Bachpan Bachao Andolan.

"We had wholeheartedly welcomed the ban because it was a step in the right direction. But it was only a step. A law is only a piece of paper if it is not enforced."

UNICEF agrees. "One year down the line, enormous challenges remain in translating that law into practice," the UN children's agency said in a statement.

Despite a ban on children under fourteen working at hazardous jobs, some children as young as nine work up to sixteen hours a day making clothing.

Some [Indian] states, particularly in the south, have been more energetic in implementing the law. Nationwide, however, only 2,229 violations of the law had been identified in the past year, leading to just 211 prosecutions of employers, according to Save the Children, quoting government data.

"What are these figures in a country the size of India? Next to nothing," Ribhu said. Official figures suggest there are around 12 million children working in India, although activists believe the real figure is closer to 60 million.

Reform Needs to Happen in Villages

For things to work better, the government needs to work backward, from the villages, said Shireen Miller of Save the Children, creating a smooth system for returning rescued children to their homes, rehabilitating them and ensuring that school places are available. These processes are not yet in place, she added.

Part of the problem is a widely shared and enduring conviction in India that child labor is not inherently wrong.

"We have yet to convince people of this," Miller said, adding that even some government ministers continued to believe that with rural poverty so extreme, employment was an acceptable solution for a child from an impoverished family.

"We need to argue that for the development and progress of the country, these children must be in education," she said.

Shantha Sinha, of the state-funded National Commission for Protection of Child Rights, concurs: "There is not enough outrage in society that these children are working and not at school. This will come only when the government begins to take serious action."

In Delhi at least, the signs are not encouraging. Ribhu said his colleagues had made repeated requests for the sweatshops of Kotla to be closed, without success. Sometimes, he said, it was that the appropriate official capable of taking action was on leave, sometimes that he was unwell, or simply out of town for a meeting,

"The information is not being acted on," he said. "It is despicable."

SEVEN

Controlling Child Labor Entails Helping Children Get an Education

Bruce Stokes

Bruce Stokes is the international economics columnist for the *National Journal*, a magazine based in Washington, DC. In this viewpoint, Stokes discusses the widespread nature of child labor, particularly in India. He cites five misconceptions that contribute to the continuation of child labor and explains why he believes they are myths. He particularly addresses the belief that child labor is a valuable part of education, claiming instead that children should be in school. He mentions governmental programs in Brazil that pay parents to send their children to school and recommends that other countries also focus their energies to create better educational opportunities for children.

The sweet-smiling young boy wearing a knit cap and rag wool sweater seemed small for his age. But then, he had lived a harder life than most 12-year-olds. Raised on the streets in rural India, he was sold by his aunt to a banker in Delhi at age 8 to work as a servant. For four years the youngster was on call 18 hours a day, scrubbing pots and cleaning house, one of the tens of thousands of Indian children now working as domestics, the new face of child labor in the country.

"The growing Indian middle class has brought this disaster to the lives of the nation's children," said Kailash Satyarthi, chairman of India's Global March Against Child Labor. As soon as they can afford them, Indian families want to acquire servants as a sign of their newfound status. And the cheapest and most docile workers available are boys and girls.

This particular child, whose identity was withheld to protect his privacy, is free now, liberated by one of Satyarthi's raid-and-rescue teams. The boy lives with three dozen other former child laborers in a community on the outskirts of India's capital. Here they receive schooling and counseling until they can be reunited with their families. And they are protected by armed guards because their former masters often try to snatch them back.

Like millions of migrants before him, this boy has no desire to return to his village. Despite the hardships he has endured, he loves the city. And, typical of children his age, he dreams. He wants to be a pilot when he grows up, although he has had only six months of education.

As unrealistic as his dream may be, it is better than the nightmare of child labor that still traps millions of other young Indians, notwithstanding a 2006 law making it illegal to employ anyone under the age of 14.

The recent decision by Primark, a low-cost British retailer, to drop three of its Indian suppliers because they subcontracted embroidery work to local firms using child labor is a harsh reminder that India still has more working children than any other country.

Another slight, dark-haired 12-year-old boy, also being sheltered at the ashram, knows the horrors of embroidery work all too well. For the last three years he embroidered suits and saris, working 16-hour days, six-and-a-half days a week alongside two dozen other children ages 8 to 16 in a New Delhi factory. He slept at his workbench. He says he was regularly beaten when his embroidery did not satisfy the owner.

"In time," the boy recalled, "my father came to the factory and asked that I be sent home. But the factory owner refused. He said, 'He has been eating a lot, and you have to pay for his sleeping arrangement, so I won't send him home.'" Eventually, Satyarthi's team liberated this boy, too. The family was given 1,500 rupees, about $35, for the boy's three years of work. (The legal minimum wage in Delhi is 4,000 rupees a month for an eight-hour day, according to Manish Sharma, manager of the ashram.)

Millions of Child Laborers Around the World

These boys are two of millions of child laborers around the world. The exact number is probably unknowable; it depends on the definition of childhood and the definition of work.

"Childhood is an evolving concept," Satyarthi said. The legal working age varies from country to country. Moreover, when it comes to farmwork and family handicraft businesses, experts differ over where to draw the line between exploitive labor and the practice of having children simply help out.

In 2004, the International Labor Organization [ILO], guesstimated that there were 218 million child laborers worldwide, seven in 10 of them working in agriculture. That figure was down 11 percent from 2000.

The Indian government admitted to 12.7 million child laborers in 2001, an increase of about 1 million in a decade. Child-labor opponents contend that the true total is more than double that figure.

In part, the increase and the discrepancy reflect the prevalence of domestic servitude, which is on the rise as Indian incomes improve. The 2001 government study estimated that the country had 185,000 domestic child workers. Activists claim that the number is much higher, noting that domestic child labor is particularly hard to document. These children work privately one and two to a household, not publicly by the dozens in factories. Many are quite young. A recent study in the southern city of Chennai found that one-quarter of child domestics began working before they were 9. More than 80 percent were girls.

"The law is being flouted behind every other door," Satyarthi said.

Five Misconceptions About Child Labor

Such child labor persists, in part, because of widespread misperceptions about its economic necessity and social benefits.

Kailash Satyarthi, chairperson of India's Global March Against Child Labor, believes that India's rising middle class has resulted in the exploitation of the nation's children, who are being pressed into labor as house servants.

Myth 1: The prevalence of child labor is an unfortunate consequence of poverty. Sri Lanka has a per capita income of $4,100, and 15 percent of its children work. India has a per capita income of $2,700, but only 6 percent of Indian children are economically active. Poor societies don't have to have child labor.

Myth 2: Children need to work to support their families. Indian surveys show that parents send their children to work believing that it will help sustain the family. But it's a bad bargain. Studies by the International Labor Organization have found that children earn about one-fifth of what adults are paid for the same work, so a child's contribution to a household is minimal at best. Moreover, premature work denies children the opportunity to acquire the skills they need to earn decent incomes as adults, undermining their ability to care for their parents in their old age. Sending one's child to work is both economically irrational and shortsighted.

Myth 3: *Curbing child labor hurts employment*. "Almost all children who work belong to those families where the parents can't

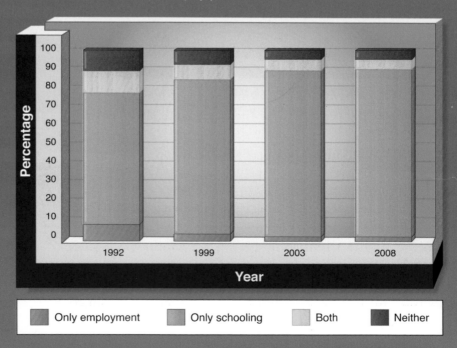

Brazilian Children Spend More Time in School

Brazilian children (aged 7–15 years) have spent increasingly less time in employment and more time in school since Brazil began to sponsor programs (the Eradication of Child Labor program (PETI) in 1996 and Bolsa Familia in 2003) that pay parents to send their children to school.

Only employment   Only schooling   Both   Neither

Taken from: *Joining Forces Against Child Labor: Interagency Report for the Hague Global Child Labour Conference of 2010.* Understanding Children's Work (UCW) Programme, International Labour Office, 2010, p.27.

find jobs for more than 100 days a year," Satyarthi said. So, many children may be taking jobs from their own parents. Despite the recent decline in child labor in India's carpet industry because of better enforcement of labor laws, and the consequent increase in labor costs, carpet exports are up and the jobs are being filled by able-bodied adults. Countries can have more jobs without employing more children.

Myth 4: Children are better suited for some work than adults. This "nimble fingers" argument is widely believed. But an ILO study of more than 2,000 weavers found that children were no more likely than adults to have the dexterity to tie the finest carpet knots. Employers just pay them less.

Myth 5: Child labor is a valuable part of early-childhood education. Studies in Brazil demonstrate that entering the workforce before age 13 can lower adult lifetime earnings as much as 17 percent. Children learn best at a desk, not at a loom.

Clearly, the eradication of child labor need not await the eradication of poverty. Brazil has shown the way. For more than a decade, the government has paid parents a small stipend—$4.50 a month per child—to send their kids to school rather than to work. More than 1 million children now participate in the program.

The ILO estimates that it would cost $38 billion a year for 20 years to eliminate child labor worldwide. Washington has already contributed more than $20 million to an Indian program to save children from the most-hazardous industries. More such investments are justified: Studies show that the economic benefits outweigh the costs by nearly 6-to-1.

In Europe and the United States, eliminating poverty did not end child labor. What made the difference was activists pressuring governments to enforce the law and to create educational opportunities for all children. That same struggle is now taking place in India. History suggests that outside pressure and financial aid can help.

"Child labor is a denial of childhood," Satyarthi said. "It's the denial of their future participation in the economy. This must end. And it is non-negotiable."

EIGHT

Ending Child Slave Labor Entails First Learning to Recognize It

Kevin Bales

Kevin Bales is an expert on modern slavery and president of an organization called Free the Slaves. In the following viewpoint taken from his book *Ending Slavery*, Bales recounts the story of a young teen who was taken from her home in Guatemala and brought to Florida where she was treated as a slave as well as raped. The girl was only discovered and rescued by an officer responding to a domestic dispute who followed up when she sensed something was not right. Bales uses this story to illustrate the importance of people's learning to look for and take notice of modern day slavery and doing something to end it.

I don't subscribe to the myth of pure evil, the idea that a slaveholder is somehow a fundamentally subhuman beast who lives only to enjoy causing suffering in others. I've met and talked with slaveholders as they played with their grandchildren or cared for their animals, and even though they are criminals who have committed terrible acts, they still seem to love their kids. I hold on to that belief because I dream of a world in which slaves are free *and* slaveholders are cured of the evil sickness of slavery as well. Still, some slaveholders make it hard to hold on to that belief, and one of these is José Tecum.

Originally from Guatemala, José Tecum lived with his wife near Naples, Florida. Having done well in America, Tecum also built himself a fine house back in his village in Guatemala. Here he lived like a prince and soon came to assume the powers of a feudal lord. Power corrupts, and the power that comes with riches in a country where even the law is for sale can warp and destroy a mind. The abuse of this power, especially to take young women for sex, is an old story. Recall the degraded villain of *Uncle Tom's Cabin*, Simon Legree, who buys young females with the intention of using them as sex slaves. Foreshadowing José Tecum, Legree takes his new fifteen-year-old slave, Emmeline, into his house to rape her and can be heard telling his distraught wife, "I'll do as I like!"

José Tecum liked Celia, a young woman in his remote village in Guatemala. We'll never know why Celia became the focus of his attention, but as Tecum watched her, he became obsessed. Celia's family was poor and dared not cross this powerful man. Still, as Tecum badgered her father to allow him to take Celia as a maid, her father continued to refuse. Finally, Tecum tried another tactic. Visiting Celia's home, he brought bottles of liquor and got her father drunk. In a drunken stupor, the father did not stop Tecum when he grabbed fifteen-year-old Celia and dragged her to the next room, where he raped her. Celia's brother cowered with his father, tortured by the shame of what was happening but feeling powerless against Tecum. The rape marked Celia by the notions of her culture as spoiled and unmarriageable. A few days later, Tecum offered money and a chance for Celia to go to America, and her family, in their shock and shame and with the fatalism of the oppressed, gave in.

Tecum had taken control of Celia's life, but before leaving for America he made his control absolute. Taking some of her hair, he performed a voodoo-like ritual that tied her to him. In Celia's village people believe that a person with enough power and the right ritual can literally take your soul. Celia believed

US Cities in Which Forced Labor Incidences Were Reported

Taken from: *Hidden Slaves: Forced Labor in the United States*. Washington, DC: Free The Slaves, 2004, p.11.

this completely. From that moment not only her present life but also her eternal life was in the hands of her rapist, and any resistance could damn her forever. To further increase his control over her, Tecum told Celia that if she crossed him, he would have her family killed.

Celia's shock increased in America. Growing up in a village with no road or cars or phones or electricity, she was baffled by many aspects of her new life. She had never seen a bridge, for example, and panicked when they drove over one in a car. Celia was isolated by language as well, normally speaking the indigenous language of her village, K'Iche, and rarely using the Spanish that most Guatemalans speak. At home in Florida, Tecum spun a tale to his wife to explain Celia—a distant relative who needed work. And at first his wife went along with this. After all, Celia was a free domestic servant, docile and obedient. When his wife left the house, Tecum did what he liked with Celia.

Unaware of Standing Next to a Slave

One day Tecum's wife came home early and found Tecum and Celia in the bedroom. She exploded, but like Simon Legree, Tecum insisted he could "do as he liked." The screaming match turned into a fight, and soon Mrs. Tecum was thrown against the wall. Injured, she managed to get to the neighbors and call the police, which in their case was the county sheriff's office. A deputy was dispatched to the scene, and he investigated and arrested Tecum on a domestic violence charge. When the deputy wrote up his report later, he mentioned that there was a young woman on the scene who was crying but that the only information he could get from her was her age—fifteen. He never realized he was standing next to a slave.

Good police and sheriff's departments have a victim assistance officer, sometimes called a victim's advocate, and the next day the local victim assistance officer paid a visit to the Tecum house. She described what she found as Mrs. Tecum opened the door:

I immediately noticed this female sitting by the window. She was dressed in her native clothes, and she appeared very sad—a very sad female.... I identified or saw that she was the same female that was talked about in the report. Then after I spoke with Mrs. Tecum, she pointed at Celia and said that it was all her fault—for sleeping with her husband.

The young woman looked terrified, and the officer sensed that something was wrong. Mrs. Tecum didn't want Celia to talk to the officer and tried to stop her, but the officer explained that it was her job to talk to everyone, and she took Celia out to the yard where they could speak by themselves. Celia told her that she wasn't in school and that

she had to work to pay Mr. Tecum 8,000 quetzal [just over $1,000]. And that's because she had to pay for the trip. At that point she started crying again, and she told me she felt like a slave. . . . She explained that all she did was work for him and that she had to obey him. She advised that she was scared of him, that all she wanted was to go back to her family in Guatemala.

Faced with a minor who "felt like a slave," who was not related to the family, who was working but not getting paid, and who was clearly distressed, the officer still wasn't sure what to do. She left and explained later:

When I left, I left kind of concerned about her statements, so then I . . . talked with the sergeant and a lieutenant, and they basically told me that they couldn't do anything and that I should just go ahead and call border patrol and have her deported. But then I immediately thought that that was not the solution for this situation, that there was something more to it.

US System Makes It Hard to Enforce Antislavery Laws

We have to admit that there was a serious flaw, not in the work of this officer but in the American law enforcement system that finds it difficult to remember and enforce our antislavery laws even when a slave stands in front of an officer and says, "I feel like a slave." We can be thankful that this woman officer bucked her superiors and kept going back to Tecum's house. She knew something was wrong but couldn't fit whatever it was into the categories provided by the system. The officer explained what happened on her fifth visit:

So at that point I went back [to Tecum's house] with the Children and Families investigator and we told Celia that she was going to go with us. . . . Mrs. Tecum became very upset. She kept talking in her dialect to Celia, intimidating her—we could notice by the body motions. A deputy was keeping Mrs. Tecum on one side while we went to assist Celia, thinking that she had a bag of clothes and everything. We were kind of surprised when we saw Celia picking up a very small plastic bag—a Winn-Dixie [supermarket chain] bag—and all she had in that bag was a pair of underwear, a pair of shoes, some sandals, and that was it. So basically the only thing she had was her native dress that she was wearing. I told her that she was going to be fine and everything; she gave me a hug, and she thanked me for taking her out.

It took five visits before Celia was brought to safety, and luckily José Tecum did not make Celia disappear after the first or second or fourth visit. If anyone deserved a hug, it was this officer, for

Kevin Bales is president of an organization called Free the Slaves. He has worked tirelessly to educate the public about child slavery and child labor.

sticking to her guns and bringing Celia to freedom. She did great work, but it wasn't on the basis of training or experience in handling slavery cases. It wasn't because her superiors were keeping her up to date on American antislavery laws. It was because her gut told her "something here is not right.". . .

Slavery in the Real World

What if a different officer had gone to Tecum's house? What if the officer had done as her superiors suggested and just had Celia deported? What if the Tecums had had the sense to hide Celia? How many of us—police, meter readers, shop workers, or hospital staff—have stood next to a slave in America (or Canada or Europe) and never known it? There are none so blind as those who will not see.

This notion of vision, of being able to see the slavery around us, is crucial. While this woman officer was straining to see the slave before her, officials in India were saying children couldn't be slaves—they were just migrant workers. Children in West Africa weren't being taken into slavery; they were being "placed" with families so they could earn a little and learn a trade, something like an apprenticeship. Those who are benefiting from slavery are creating smoke screens to obscure our vision; most of the rest of us just live in a fog of ignorance. Is it any surprise that the crime of slavery is wrapped in many layers of rationalizations, justifications, and plain bald lies? Part of our job is to pierce this fog of lies and ignorance and to recognize the slavery around us whether in our own communities or in other countries. Later, the woman officer said that building up an understanding of Celia's case was "like starting from zero." So it is with most of us; we abhor the idea of slavery, but we're not sure what it looks like in the real world.

NINE

Faith-Based Efforts Can Help End Child Slave Labor

Deann Alford

> At the time this viewpoint was written, Deann Alford was a writer for *Christianity Today*. The viewpoint tells how Sandy Shepherd, a Baptist woman from Texas, got involved with helping to free slaves who have been trafficked into the United States illegally and forced to work under inhumane conditions. Shepherd's church had previously hosted a boys' choir from Zambia, not realizing at that time that the boys were being treated as slaves. When she later received a call that the boys were being deported, she agreed to help. Eventually she and her husband adopted one of the boys. Mother and adopted son have since been working together to defend the rights of trafficked slaves.

Seven years ago, Sandy Shepherd got an unexpected phone call as she headed to her daughter's high school musical rehearsal. A mother of three, living in affluent Colleyville near Fort Worth [Texas], she was already beginning to imagine life as an empty nester. She wasn't thinking about changing the world.

On the line was Deacon Neel Choate from her church, First Baptist. He told her that the Immigration and Naturalization Service (INS) had just picked up seven Zambian boys—all part of a touring choir they both knew. First Baptist had hosted the choir previously. Choate said the boys needed a place to stay or they would spend the night in jail. Could she house all seven overnight?

Shepherd took a deep breath. For two years, Shepherd had passionately supported this choir, utterly unaware that she and her church were being duped.

A Baptist missionary, Keith Grimes, had recruited the boys to tour America with his ministry, TTT: Partners in Education. Grimes had made big promises to the boys and their families. He had inspired them with talk of salaries, an American education, and stipends for families back in Zambia. Grimes had also claimed the tour would raise money for Kalingalinga, the grindingly poor shantytown that provided its fresh-faced sons for these tours 6,000 miles from their homes.

It was a brilliant scam. The ministry never paid these Zambian boys a dime or built new schools. It pocketed all the sponsorship money.

When the fraud was discovered, Shepherd and others had done everything they could to stop it, but had failed. Not even Grimes's 1999 death had ended the boys' enslavement. His kin took over and kept the captive choir out on the road. The boys spoke little English. Their mother tongue had no word for *slave*.

By the time of Deacon Choate's phone call, Shepherd was disengaged from the choir. She had channeled her outrage into outreach. She had joined other American Christians aware of the scheme, and they had built a village school, using their own resources even as Grimes's deception continued.

In January 2000, the choir scam imploded. After the boys sang in a Houston church, they quit in disgust and exhaustion. Their manager telephoned the INS, demanding their immediate deportation to Zambia.

A Reluctant Liberator

How could Shepherd now invest more emotional capital in this tragic mess she'd already failed to defuse? She answered Choate with hesitation in her voice: "I don't know if I want to get back involved in this."

Choate laid out the boys' plight. The teens had done no-thing wrong. The INS only had housing available in a federal jail. Could she meet him at 7 at the church?

Shepherd sighed. "I guess I'll be there," she said.

As Shepherd drove her van to her church through spotless neighborhoods of Texas-sized trophy houses, she begged God: "Lord, I don't want to be involved in this anymore. Why are you calling me back?"

A song she sang in First Baptist's choir popped into her head: "Yes, Lord, yes, I will answer the call."

That night, the seven choristers slept in her home, and the course of her family's life was changed forever—especially through the Shepherds' relationship with Given Kachepa, then a skinny 13-year-old orphan.

Days later, TTT staff began peppering the Shepherd house-hold with aggressive phone calls concerning the fate of the boys. Nobody was safe. The couple found other hosts. But Kachepa was soon homeless again. Without hesitation this time, Sandy and her husband, Deetz, took him in and enrolled him in the eighth grade. During the following years, the Shepherds included him in every family portrait, paid for braces on his teeth, and coached him through high school and into college.

These days, Kachepa and Shepherd are an unlikely duo: a freed modern-day slave and his reluctant liberator. They travel nation-ally, advising other victims of human trafficking, pushing lawmak-ers to make enforcement of antislavery laws a true priority, and speaking at antislavery events.

They combat an ancient scourge that has never really gone away. Two hundred years after William Wilberforce campaigned to abolish the slave trade within the British Empire, slavery con-tinues. Experts estimate there are 27 million slaves worldwide today, probably more than at any time in human history. About 17,000 are trafficked annually into the United States.

"They are not slaves in a metaphorical sense," notes International Justice Mission founder Gary Haugen. "They are held in forced servitude by other human beings."

Shepherd, Kachepa, and Haugen are part of an alliance of modern Wilberforces. This alliance is both ordinary and extraordinary—each person deeply challenged by modern slavery and willing to pay the high price of personal involvement.

Their ranks include lawmakers, clergy, lawyers, bureaucrats, missionaries, social workers, and even reclusive Colorado billionaire Philip Anschutz. He bankrolled the new feature film *Amazing Grace*, which chronicles Wilberforce's life....

Victims Should Not Be Treated Like Criminals

Illicit sex dominates public awareness of modern-day slavery. For years, when local police arrested a prostituted woman who was an illegal alien, she was deported. It was the perfect cover for sex traffickers and their clients. The state punished the victim, unaware of her enslavement.

International traffickers set up elaborate, clandestine pipelines to transport women and children thousands of miles to sustain the global sex industry. Experts now understand that these pipelines involve people from at least 150 nations. Existing laws criminalized fraud, unpaid labor, battery, extortion, rape, and related crimes. Laws that criminalized the trafficking pipeline were absent, however.

To stop slavery, faith-based and secular activists realized that national governments had to radically reorient their view of people who were trafficked. This realization set in motion one of the new abolitionist movement's most stunning legislative success stories of the last 20 years. In the late 1990s, Rep. Chris Smith, R-N.J., and Sen. Sam Brownback, R-Kan., worked with anti-slavery groups to enact the Trafficking Victims Protection Act (TVPA). President [Bill] Clinton, despite his initial resistance, signed the legislation in October 2000. In the U.S. alone, the new legislation and tough enforcement triggered an 800 percent increase in the number of federal trafficking cases during a five-year period.

The TVPA, strengthened in 2003 and 2005, fits sharp new teeth on existing state and federal laws. It criminalizes each element in the trafficking pipeline, from the country of origin (such as Thailand), to the so-called transit country (like Mexico or Greece), to the destination country (pehaps the U.S. or Europe).

Sandy Shepherd, left, and husband, Deetz, pose with a young Zambian orphan, Given Kachepa, whom they rescued from slave traffickers. Sandy worked with a religious group to rescue a boys choir (that included Kachepa) from indentured servitude.

Those convicted of involvement in any part of the pipeline can face a life sentence in prison.

The Zambian choir case illustrates how difficult it was to prosecute modern slavery prior to the TVPA law.

Choirboys Who Disobeyed Were Deported

In 1993, when Grimes visited Kalingalinga, he heard about its great pride: its singing boys. He auditioned scores of them to form a choir to tour the United States. He called it the Zambian Acappella Boys Choir (ZABC).

In August 1996, First Baptist Colleyville hosted the debut of a new 26-voice group. Choristers stayed with Sandy and Deetz Shepherd. Sandy arranged performances in public schools and churches.

In less than a year, the boys picked up enough English to defy Grimes. They confided in their hosts, telling them the staff stole gifts of cash and phone cards. They described grueling workdays with up to seven 60-minute concerts per day.

The choir generated huge donations. One ministry budget statement that [*Christianity Today*] obtained reveals that the choir in one year brought in $1 million.

The ministry contract contained many loopholes and tough restrictions: "Full education at home in a boarding school only if the team works together with TTT to accomplish this project." Another: "I will complete my fall choir schedule and not complain about what is requested to complete the job." Failure to comply resulted in the chorister's return to Zambia without payment.

Health care was denied them. Defiant Louisiana hosts took an ill chorister to a doctor. The child had active tuberculosis [TB]. Health officials tested the whole group, and 21 of 26 skin-tested positive for TB.

On Christmas Eve 1997, Grimes told Shepherd he planned to return eight boys to Zambia for being "troublemakers." Grimes had fresh voices from Kalingalinga ready to replace them. Among them, was orphaned Given Kachepa, who lived in his aunt's one-room shack.

"In Zambia [Grimes] was an angel," Kachepa said. "This was the man who was going to change Kalingalinga." Kachepa's aunt gladly signed his contract, even though she couldn't read English.

In May 1998, First Baptist curtailed its support. Meanwhile, activists Janet Tyson and Kathy Helm King (Methodists from

Lake Dallas, Texas) detailed Grimes's abuses in letters to then Attorney General Janet Reno and other state and federal agencies.

What happened was worse than nothing: An FBI agent visited the boys. "At the time, it didn't meet their definition of slavery," Tyson [states], "because the boys weren't shackled."

After Grimes died in April 1999, his daughter and her husband assumed control. The daughter demanded that federal agents jail two choirboys for being a "physical threat." Officers handcuffed them, but then released them and opened an investigation.

After a January 2000 concert in Houston, the seven remaining choristers told Grimes's daughter to pay their wages or call the INS to take them away. She drove them back to TTT's compound in Sherman, Texas, and called the feds.

Eventually, the Department of Labor filed suit against TTT: Partners in Education. On December 4, 2000, federal Judge Paul Brown signed a $966,000 judgment by default against TTT, Grimes's widow, their daughter Barbara I. Martens, and her husband, Gary, for back wages and overtime for 67 choristers from November 1, 1996, through May 1, 1999. In a *Dallas Morning News* article on Brown's ruling, Barbara Martens was quoted [as] saying the boys were "volunteers."

In the six and a half years since the Grimeses' case and passage of the TVPA, the U.S. and other nations, with the support of the U.N., have aggressively cracked down on human trafficking. Federal agencies report:

- A 170 percent increase in convictions worldwide for trafficking over a three-year period starting in 2003. In 2005, global convictions totaled 4,766.
- An 871 percent increase in U.S. prosecutions for trafficking from 2001 to 2005 compared to the previous five years (1996 to 2000).
- 1,189 special T visas issued to foreign-born victims of trafficking or family members, allowing them legal residence. (Up to 5,000 T visas per year are allowed.)

- Designation of 12 countries as "Tier 3" nations. These countries do not comply with antislavery laws. The governments of North Korea and Burma, for example, are actively engaged in human trafficking.

Recently, Ambassador John R. Miller, the first person to head the federal Office to Monitor and Combat Trafficking in Persons, stepped down. Before he left office, he handed out special "New Abolitionist" awards to a handful of activists, including Janice Crouse of Concerned Women for America. On a recent radio broadcast, Crouse said, "It pleases me immensely that those of us of the evangelical faith are right there on the front lines and have been acknowledged as leaders in the abolitionist movement.". . .

Freed Slaves Take Time to Heal

Since the enslaved choir disbanded, Kachepa and other choristers have struggled to remake their lives. A few of them still tour in the U.S. as the Zambian Vocal Group and Zambian Vocal Collection.

Zambian families who expected their children to return rich are still destitute, and lingering conflict has splintered homes. But some former hosts have adopted choir members, and other choristers have married Americans. Arkansas physicians sponsored one choirboy through medical school. Now he's a doctor in Florida. With help from Shepherd and others, 17 former choristers have received T visas.

Kachepa can never return to Zambia. Corrupt government officials he exposed and envious former choristers have vowed to kill him.

[Kevin] Bales of Free the Slaves [reports] that activist Shepherd is a typical antislavery crusader. She is an everyday citizen who would not let injustice prevail and was willing to risk personal involvement. "She understands it's not just about one boy," Bales said. "It's got to be about the thousands of people who are in the same situation.

"She does it just doggedly. She's warm, friendly, loving, and relentless."

Benefits Under the Trafficking Victims Protection Reauthorization Act

Victims of human trafficking that have been declared eligible for benefits under the Trafficking Victims Protection Reauthorization Act (TVPRA) include both adults and children.

Fiscal Year	Minors	Adults	Total
2001	4	194	198
2002	18	81	99
2003	6	145	151
2004	16	147	163
2005	34	197	231
2006	20	214	234
2007	33	270	303
2008	31	286	317
2009	50	330	380
Total	**212**	**1864**	**2076**

Taken from: *Attorney General's Annual Report to Congress and Assessment of US Government Activities to Combat Trafficking in Persons*, Fiscal Year 2009, US Department of Justice, 2010.

A T visa is valid for three years. Though recipients may apply for permanent residency after that, the first recipients of T visas are almost two years overdue for receiving permanent residency. Red tape and security concerns are putting their lives in a holding pattern.

Once Given Kachepa receives permanent residency, he hopes to have a reunion outside Zambia with his family. He has worked three jobs to support kin he last saw half his life ago. Enrolled in college, he aspires to study dentistry. Kachepa's antislavery work earned him a 2006 "Teen That Is Going to Change the World" recognition from *Teen People* magazine.

But a rosy future is hard to come by for many enslaved persons. "Most people who are trafficked into the United States we never know anything about," Bales said.

Behind her foster son's captivating smile, Shepherd notes a deep sadness. Drop-dead handsome, yet humble, Kachepa's spirit seems dogged by survivor's guilt—ever mindful of God's blessing, yet burdened to help others.

He yearns to move on. "I don't like my identity—being known as a trafficking victim," Kachepa said. "That's why I'm working so hard, so I can create my own identity."

At First Baptist Colleyville on a Sunday last October, Kachepa and his American parents heard a guest pastor's sermon on how to heal a broken heart.

"God will use your scars and your pain to bring blessing to others," said David Allen, dean of theology at Southwestern Baptist Theological Seminary in Fort Worth. "Only God can bring a ministry on the other side of a broken heart. Jesus will heal your broken heart, if you'll bring all the pieces to him."

Even broken Christians may bring moral authority and grassroots strength to the new abolition movement. "That combination has been potent," said Allen D. Hertzke, director of religious studies at the University of Oklahoma and author of *Freeing God's Children: The Unlikely Alliance for Global Human Rights*.

"There's no question in my mind that without the Christian community, [the TVPA] would not have passed."

Bales believes the actions of ordinary citizens have freed about one-third of the former slaves in the United States.

But the quest cannot end there. "We now have one of the best laws in the whole world," Bales said. "We have to spend the money to enforce that law and train police how to use it."

Wilberforce's work remains unfinished. Today's church is returning to a historic labor.

"God hates slavery," Bales said. "We're going to make sure the gift we give—not to each other but to God—is an end to this slavery."

TEN

Child Labor Can Be Controlled Through Unionizing

Nick Logan

> Nick Logan worked as a web reporter for the sixty-eighth global voyage of the Japan-based Peace Boat, a chartered passenger ship that travels around the world to promote peace and human rights. In this viewpoint, Logan describes how Peruvian children explained their labor organizations to their Japanese visitors. In Peru, many children work to support their families. Rather than fighting to abolish child labor, two Peruvian organizations, the Movement of Adolescent and Child Workers, Children of Christian Laborers and the National Movement of Organized Child and Adolescent Workers of Peru, endeavor to ensure that children work no more than four hours per day under good working conditions and that they also receive a good education.

"What laws do you have in Japan to protect working children?" asked a teenaged Peruvian girl. The group of guests from Peace Boat sat silent for a few moments before one participant explained that most young people in Japan don't work unless they're trying to earn money for things such as clothes and cell phones. The girl and her friends appeared slightly surprised at the response; for them, a job isn't a privilege.

Nick Logan, "Peace Boat 68th Global Voyage Report: Rights for Peru's Child Labourers," nickaroundtheworld.wordpress.com and peaceboat.org, April 2010 © Nick Logan/Peace Boat. All rights reserved. Reproduced by permission.

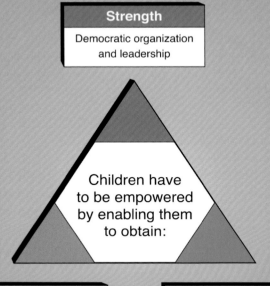

Empowering Children Gives Them More Control over Labor Conditions

Strength
Democratic organization and leadership

Children have to be empowered by enabling them to obtain:

Information
Ownership of information, access to analysis, and use of information

Resources
Access to and use of financial, human, and material resources

Taken from: The Concerned for Working Children, *Journey in Children's Participation,* compiled and edited by Nandana Reddy and Kavita Ratna, December 2002, p. 37.

Organisations around the world try to ensure children don't have to start working at a young age, but the reality is that some children must earn money to support themselves or their families. Children in Lima and throughout Peru work in factories, shops and internet cafes, or at markets; some have to sell snacks on buses or work on the streets playing music or washing car windows. Unfortunately, many youngsters don't know their rights or have the education to seek out employment where they're not exploited and underpaid.

With the assistance of MANTHOC [Spanish initialism standing for Movement of Adolescent and Child Workers, Children for Christian Laborers] and MNNATSOP [Spanish initialism for National Movement of Organized Child and Adolescent Workers of Peru] partner organisations with centers located all over the country—children and adolescents are standing up for their dignity and safety and learning skills to find jobs that offer sufficient pay. "There are laws in Peru about child workers," says Olga Rivera Roman. "(They) only refer to children over the age of 14, but in reality there are children younger than that who are working." Ms Rivera has worked with MANTHOC for 15 years and is currently president of the association, which actively works with more than 3000 young people nation-wide. In Peru, she explains, there are more than 2.5 million child labourers, and many of them work in "precarious" situations.

Kids Work to Help Their Families

Fifteen-year-old Stefany, a junior high school student who works as a vendor, extended a warm welcome to 68th voyage participants at the MANTHOC center in the Amauta A district of Lima, and offered the group of 35 visitors some insight into [the organization's] situation.

"Kids work because our families don't have money," she says, "so we need to support them . . . and improve our quality of life." According to Ms Rivera, families in Amauta generally live on $100–150 USD a month, earned by the parents, which is not nearly enough to support an entire family.

In more than three decades of work, MANTHOC—a Christian organisation—has given these children a voice and brought them into the public eye, encouraging them to push society to change how it treats child labourers. The NGO [nongovernmental organization] strives to make sure children who must work do so in adequate conditions—for no more than four hours a day—safe from mistreatment and abuse (both physical and sexual). The other important goal, Ms Rivera says, is guaranteeing that the children still have the opportunity to go to school and study.

The organisation itself offers specialized education programmes and job training workshops. A small number of children can also work for MANTHOC through alternative work projects, making fair-trade goods—sold in Peru and internationally—as well as in one of the hostels the organisation has set up.

Partner-organisation MNNATSOP formed in 1996 as [a] spin-off from MANTHOC, in conjunction with other child labour groups. While the goals and activities are quite similar, the younger, secular organisation has grown so large it now assists more than 14,000 children, including those living on the streets.

"(They) organise the children who work so that in the future we don't face exploitation," says MNNATSOP and MANTHOC member Samuel, age 15. "We can't wait for the future for our rights. We need society to protect our rights now."

MNNATSOP conducts major campaigns for children's rights, including the ¡Más Respeto! (More Respect!) campaign which aims for global recognition of child workers and the contributions they make to society. Each year the world marks International Worker's Day on May 1, but this is an acknowledgement of adult labourers; MNNATSOP wants children to be included as well. The organisation wrote in a 2008 newsletter that studies suggest children and adolescents contributed one per cent to Peru's Gross Domestic Product (GDP), but their labour doesn't figure into statistics.

Peruvian Children Receive Support

Before arriving at the port of Callao, guest educator Yoshii Yutaka—a freelance photographer living in Lima—introduced Peru's child labour issue to 68th voyage participants and told them of a Japanese connection to MNNATSOP: the legacy of Nagayama Norio. Mr Nagayama was born into severe poverty in post-war northern Japan. His family was so poor that his father died in a ditch in winter when Norio was only five, and his mother abandoned [the child]. After moving to Tokyo as a teenager and continuing to live in poverty, he murdered four people in 1968. He argued, before being sentenced to death, his harsh living

The Movement of Adolescent and Child Workers, Children for Christian Laborers strives to ensure that Peruvian children work no more than four hours a day in good conditions and that they have time to attend school and study.

conditions led him to his fate. He wasn't executed until 1997, but in prison he wrote novels about his life and hardships. Mr Nagayama originally used the money from his book sales to compensate his victims' families. After 28 years in prison he was put to death by hanging, and at that time he decided to leave what savings he had to help prevent other disadvantaged children from winding up like him. With the help of people such as Mr Yoshii, MNNATSOP received support from Mr Nagayama's estate.

Child Soldiers Are a New Phenomenon

P.W. Singer

P.W. Singer is a leading expert on twenty-first-century warfare. In this viewpoint, he discusses modern changes that he believes have made this century the first in history in which children have been used as soldiers on such a global scale. These changes include poverty, which encourages children to join the military for a sense of power and stability, and technology, which has made weapons that are simple to use, even by a child. Singer declares that it is immoral to recruit children to fight in adult wars and expresses hope that this period in history will be short-lived.

"I was attending primary school." The young boy speaks in a monotone; masking his emotions as he recounts events that irrevocably changed his life. "The rebels came and attacked us. They killed my mother and father in front of my eyes. I was 10 years old. They took me with them."

The boy, now 16, lives in a refugee camp in his native Liberia, a small nation in West Africa. Liberia was founded in 1821 on the hopes of freed American slaves, but by the dawn of the 21st century the country had dissolved into brutal, warlord-driven civil strife that left more than 200,000 dead. One feature of that

P.W. Singer, "Children at War," *Military History*, September 2007, pp. 50–55. Copyright © 2007 by Weider History Group. All rights reserved. Reproduced by permission.

conflict is that rebel and government forces alike have abducted some 20,000 Liberian children, forcing many of them into front-line combat.

"They trained us to fight," the boy continues. "The first time I killed someone, I got sick. I thought I was going to die. But I got better. . . . My fighting name was Blood Never Dry."

Only Recently Have Children Fought in Wars

When we think of fighting wars, children rarely come to mind. War is the province of strong and willing adult combatants, from which the young, the old, the infirm and the innocent are to be protected. Exclusion of children from direct and deliberate participation in war has been observed in almost every culture. Warriors typically joined precolonial African armies several years after puberty. In the Zulu tribe, for example, it was not until the ages of 18 to 20 that members were eligible for *ukubuthwa* (draft or enrollment into tribal regiments). In the Kano region of West Africa, only married men were conscripted—unmarried men were considered too immature. When children did serve in ancient armies, such as the enrollment of Spartan children in military training at ages 7 to 9, they typically did not see combat. Instead, they [did] menial chores: herding cattle, bearing shields and mats for senior warriors. No traditional tribes or ancient civilizations included young boys or girls in their fighting forces.

Exclusion of children from war was simply pragmatic. Adult strength and lengthy training were required to master premodern weapons like swords and longbows. Age restrictions also enabled rules and elders to maintain control of their younger—and potentially unruly—subjects.

As in Sparta, there were occasions in military history where children proved useful. Boy pages helped arm and maintain the knights of medieval Europe. Drummer boys and "powder monkeys," small boys who ran ammunition to cannon crews, were a requisite part of armies and navies in the 17th and 18th centuries. However, these youths were not true combatants. They neither dealt out death nor were considered legitimate targets. Henry V was so angered by the slaying of English boy pages at the 1415 Battle of Agincourt that he, in turn, slaughtered his French prisoners.

Perhaps the best-known early use of "child soldiers" occurred during the 1212 Children's Crusade, a march of thousands of unarmed boys from northern France and western Germany when [it was] thought they might take back the Holy Land by the sheer power of their faith. Most never left Europe. Of those who did, all but a few perished from hunger and disease or were sold into slavery by unscrupulous ships' captains.

Few Exceptions

Until recently, there have been few exceptions to the practice of keeping children from combat. Underage boys have certainly lied about their age to join armies in many places and wars, and a few modern states—desperate and facing defeat—have sent children into battle. In America, the most notable instance of youths in combat was the participation by Virginia Military Institute [VMI] cadets in the Battle of New Market, in May 1864. Union forces had marched up the Shenandoah Valley, hoping to cut the Virginia Central railroad, a key supply line. Facing them, Confederate General John C. Breckenridge had pulled together some 5,000 men, including cadets from nearby VMI. Two hundred forty-seven students, aged 15 to 17, waited until the final stages of battle. Then, in a dramatic charge, they overran a key Union artillery battery. Ten cadets were killed and 45 were wounded.

In World War II, the *Hitler Jugend* (Hitler Youth) received quasi-military training, then joined the German military forces, often the SS, once they reached age 18. But in the final months of the war, even the boys were ordered to fight in a desperate gamble to hold off Allied troops until new "miracle" weapons like a V-2 rocket and Me-262 jet fighters could turn the tide. Lightly armed and often sent out in ambush squads, scores of Hitler Youth members were killed in small-scale skirmishes. Such episodes were only isolated footnotes to military history. But in recent decades, that pattern has changed.

Children and the Changed Nature of War

As the nature of armed conflict has changed in recent years, the practice of using children—defined under international law as those under age 18—as soldiers has become far more common and widespread. As many as 300,000 children 17 and under now serve worldwide as combatants. They fight in about 75 percent of the world's conflicts. In the last 10 years [1998–2007], children have served as soldiers on every continent but Antarctica, with

Some twenty thousand Liberian children were abducted by rebel and government forces alike and forced to become soldiers.

the largest numbers in Asia and Africa. Moreover, an additional half-million children serve in armed forces that are now at war.

These are not youngsters on the cusp of adulthood. Eighty percent of the conflicts in which children participate include fighters 14 and under, while 18 percent of the world's armed organizations have used children 12 and under. The average age of child soldiers in two recent studies, one in Southeast Asia and one in Central Africa, was just under 13. The youngest recorded child soldier was an armed 5-year-old in Uganda.

Girl Soldiers

The presence of girls as combatants in many forces also deviates from historic trends. While no girls served as Civil War powder monkeys or in groups like the Hitler Youth, roughly 30 percent of the armed forces that employ children today include girl soldiers. Underage girls have participated in the armed forces of 55 countries; in 34 of these, girls saw combat, and in 27 nations they were abducted to serve. Girl soldiers are often singled out for sexual abuse, even by their own commanders, and have a harder time integrating back into society at war's end.

With the spread of such practices, Western conventional military forces have increasingly come into conflict with child soldiers. During Operation Barras in Sierra Leone in 2000, British troops fought a pitched battle against the West Side Boys, a teen militia that had taken hostage a squad of British army troops. As one observer noted, "You cannot resolve a situation like this with a laser-guided bomb from 30,000 feet." In that battle, one British soldier was killed and 12 were wounded. Estimates of casualties among the West Side Boys ranged from 25 up to 150.

Today, child soldiers are present in every conflict, some where U.S. forces operate, from Afghanistan to the Philippines. The first U.S. soldier killed in the War on Terrorism was a Green Beret shot by a 14-year-old sniper in Afghanistan. During the initial fighting in Afghanistan, U.S. forces captured some half-dozen boys aged 13 to 16. They were taken to Guantánamo Bay, Cuba, and housed in a special wing dubbed Camp Iguana, where they spent their days in a beach house converted into a makeshift prison, watching DVDs and learning English and math. U.S. soldiers continue to report facing child soldiers in Afghanistan. The youngest on record is a 12-year-old boy captured last year [2006] after being wounded during a Taliban ambush of a convoy.

Child Terrorists

Captured al Qaeda training videos reveal young boys receiving instruction in the manufacture of bombs and the setting of explosive booby traps. The Palestinian groups Islamic Jihad and Hamas have recruited children as young as 13 to be suicide bombers and children as young as 11 to smuggle explosives and weapons. At least 30 suicide bombing attacks have been carried out by youths since Israeli-Palestinian fighting flared up in 2000. Perhaps the most tragic example was a semi-retarded 16-year-old boy whom Hamas convinced to strap on explosives. Israeli security forces in the town of Nablus stopped the boy as he was about to blow himself up at an army checkpoint.

Children's participation in terrorism is not a uniquely Middle Eastern phenomenon, however. In Colombia, a 9-year-old boy was sent by ELN [National Liberation Army] rebels to bomb a polling station in 1997. Sri Lanka's Liberation Tigers of Tamil Eelam (aka Tamil Tigers) have even manufactured specialized denim jackets in children's sizes to conceal suicide explosives.

Three Intertwined Forces

The widespread presence of child soldiers on the 21st-century battlefield stems from three intertwined forces. First is the social and economic disruption caused by globalization. We are living through the most prosperous period in human history, yet many are being left behind. Demographic changes, global social instability and the legacy of multiple civil and sectarian conflicts entering their second and third generations all act to weaken states and undermine societal structures. For example, more than 40 million African children will lose one or both of their parents to HIV-AIDS by 2010, while the office of the United Nations High

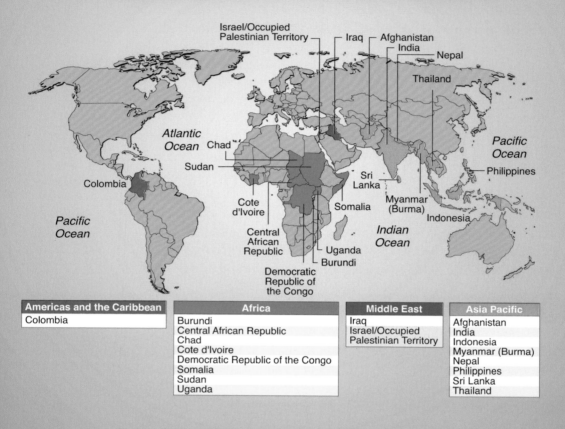

Countries/Situations Where Children Were Recruited or Used in Hostilities— April 2004 to October 2007

Americas and the Caribbean	Africa	Middle East	Asia Pacific
Colombia	Burundi Central African Republic Chad Cote d'Ivoire Democratic Republic of the Congo Somalia Sudan Uganda	Iraq Israel/Occupied Palestinian Territory	Afghanistan India Indonesia Myanmar (Burma) Nepal Philippines Sri Lanka Thailand

Taken from: Coalition to Stop the Use of Child Soldiers, *Child Soldiers: Global Report 2008*, p. 4.

Commissioner for Refugees (UNHCR) estimates that more than 2.3 million children worldwide are now homeless war refugees. Orphans and refugee children are particularly at risk of being pulled into war.

Second, changes in weapons technology have acted as an enabler, making heavily armed child warriors a practicality. The proliferation of light, simple and cheap small arms, like the "child-portable" AK-47 [assault rifle], has made them widely available for the price of a goat or chicken in many countries. They are easy enough to use that a child can manage them, and with just a half hour's instruction, a 10-year-old can wield the fire-power of a 19th-century infantry company.

Third, we are living in an exceptional period of flux and break-down of global order, marked in some regions by failed states and the spread of warlordism. Armed conflicts are now driven less by national politics than by religious hatred, ethnic strife or personal profit (e.g., the fighting over diamond mines in parts of Africa). From Foday Sankhoh in Sierra Leone to Mullah Omar in Afghanistan, local warlords see the advantages in converting vulnerable, disconnected children into low-cost and expendable troops who fight and die for their causes. Such groups' recruiting practices take advantage of children's desperation, vulnerability and immaturity. Some simply resort to kidnapping.

Why Children Become Soldiers

Those of us living in stable, wealthy nations may have difficulty understanding how a child can be convinced to join an army. But imagine yourself as an orphan living on the street, not knowing where your next meal will come from, and an organized group of adults offers you not only food and safety, but an identity, as well as the empowerment that comes from having a gun in your hand. Imagine the temptation if a group of older boys wearing natty uniforms and cool sunglasses were to show up at your school and force all the teachers to bow down to show who is "really in charge," then invite you to join them with the promise that you too can wield such power. Or imagine what happened to a 7-year-old boy in Liberia when a group of armed men showed up at his village. "The rebels told me to join them, but I said no," he later recalled. "Then they killed my smaller brother. I changed my mind."

Recruits are run through training programs that range from weeks of adult-style boot camp to a few minutes instruction in how to fire a gun. Indoctrination, political or religious, can include such "tests" as forcing the kids to kill animals or human prisoners to inure them to the sight of blood and death. Many are forced to take drugs to further desensitize them. Corrine Dufka, of Human Rights Watch, described the process in West Africa: "It seemed to be a very organized strategy of . . . breaking down their defenses and memory and turning them into fighting machines that didn't have a sense of empathy and feeling for the civilian population." The result is that children, even those who were once unwilling captives, are turned into fierce, skilled fighters.

Battlefield Ramifications

The battlefield ramifications of this child soldier doctrine are sobering, as rebels and fringe armies can field far greater forces than previously possible. Groups little larger than gangs can sustain themselves as viable military threats. The Lord's Resistance Army in Uganda, led by Joseph Kony, for instance, has with just 200 adult core members abducted more than 14,000 children, using them to fight a decade-long civil war against the Ugandan army, one of the better forces in Africa at a cost of 100,000 dead and 500,000 refugees. Kony sees himself as the reincarnation of the Christian Holy Spirit, with a warped spin on the Ten Commandments [that] allows the ownership of sex slaves but declares that riding bicycles is a sin punishable by death.

Experiences from around the globe show that child combatants can operate with terrifying audacity, particularly when infused with religious or political fervor or under the influence of drugs. A former Green Beret once described a unit of child soldiers in Sudan as the best he had seen in Africa in his 18 years there, recounting how they were able to ambush and shoot down a Soviet-made M1-24 attack helicopter. . . .

For the child soldiers, the impact of being plunged into war creates problems long after the end of actual combat. Many suffer long-term trauma that can disrupt their development. For a society at large, conversion of a generation of children into soldiers not only precipitates future cycles of war within the country, but also threatens regional stability. Throughout the 1990s, Liberia went through multiple rounds of civil war at which children haphazardly switched sides. After the fighting ended, many former child soldiers went on to fight in Sierra Leone, Guinea and the Ivory Coast. Some marched thousands of miles to find work as soldiers in Congo.

Recruiting Children as Soldiers Is Immoral

It is immoral that adults should want children to fight their wars for them. Nobel Peace Prize winner Archbishop Desmond Tutu [of South Africa] said, "There is simply no excuse, no acceptable argument for arming children." One solution to this practice lies in shrinking the pool of potential child recruits and limiting conflict groups' willingness and ability to access it. Possible preventive measures include: greater aid to at-risk groups like refugees and AIDS orphans; curbing the spread of illegal small arms; preparing regular adult soldiers to effectively deal with the threat in the field; prosecuting leaders who abuse children; sanctioning firms or regimes that trade with child soldier groups; investment to head off global disease and conflict outbreaks; and increasing aid to programs that seek to demobilize and rehabilitate former child soldiers.

Perhaps history will look back upon this period as an aberration, a phase when moral norms broke down but were then restored. That will only happen if we match the will of those who do such evil to children with our own will to do good.

TWELVE

Child Soldiers Are Not a New Phenomenon

David Rosen

David Rosen is an American anthropologist and professor. In this viewpoint, he states that in many instances child soldiers are not victims, as some scholars and humanitarians claim, but choose to fight for something they believe in. He uses the American Civil War, where at least ten thousand boys under the age of eighteen fought, as a historical example. He also cites several modern instances where children have fought honorably, such as the Jewish youth resistance during World War II, which fought against the Nazis. He questions whether child soldiers should be considered victims or heroes.

The presence of child soldiers in small-scale conflicts throughout the world has become a global humanitarian crisis and a media sensation. Television and magazines supply pumped-up images of cigar-smoking, gun-toting 11-year-olds while official reports from the United Nations and a host of human rights organizations expose alarming details of what is usually described as a "growing phenomenon." But is this really something new?

Contradictory Images of Child Soldiers

Humanitarian organizations and the news media offer up two seemingly contradictory images of child soldiers: one, as exploited

David Rosen, "Child Soldiers, Victims or Heroes?" *FDU Magazine*, Summer/Fall, 2005, Copyright © FDU Magazine. All rights reserved. Reproduced by permission.

victims of adult abuse of power and, two, as enraged, virtually uncontrollable killers. (The term "child soldier," as used here, refers to those below the age of 18.) There are many examples. Ismael Baeh, a child soldier forcibly recruited into the Sierra Leone army at age 14, described his recruitment as follows: "I either had to join the Sierra Leone army or be killed—it was the only way to survive and to be alive. First of all they gave me a brief training in how to use a weapon, a G-3 gun. Next thing you knew you were on the front line. . . . When we got there we were in an ambush—the rebels were attacking where we were in the bush. I did not shoot my gun at first—but when you looked around and saw your schoolmates younger than you, crying while they were dying . . . there was no option but to start pulling the trigger."

Baeh's narrative of victimization and abuse at the hands of the Sierra Leone army was used by the Coalition to Stop the Use of Child Soldiers to launch its *Global Report 2001* on child soldiers. But it is not the only story of child soldiers. Sebastian Junger's account of the battle for Freetown [capital of Sierra Leone] takes a decidedly darker turn. "War," Junger tells us [in a 2000 article in *Vanity Fair*], "does not get worse than on January 6, 1999. Teenage soldiers out of their minds on drugs rounded up entire neighborhoods and machine-gunned them or burned them alive in their homes. . . . They killed people who refused to give them money, or people who didn't give them enough money, or people who looked at them wrong. . . . They favored Tupac T-shirts and fancy haircuts and . . . had been fighting since they were 8 or 9, some of them, and sported names such as Colonel Bloodshed, Commander Cut Hands, Superman, Mr. Die, and Captain Backblast."

These two descriptions of children at war—on the face of it so different from one another—are in fact part of the same representation of children: a depiction that denies children social and moral agency or accountability. Monster or victim, contemporary images of child soldiers are filled with allusions to the children of [the movie] *Village of the Damned* or [the novel] *Lord of the Flies*. Their power for good and evil lies outside them—either in the alien invaders of their bodies, their drug-crazed minds or in their regression to unsocialized unmediated evil. The broadcasting of stock-in-trade images of evil children drawn from western horror narratives should at least give us pause. These depictions of children as angels or demons tell us very little about children or about the wars in which they participate.

The Crisis May Not Be Real

To assess the situation, one first needs to look at the question of whether the child soldier crisis is really a crisis at all, and whether it is as novel a phenomenon as humanitarian groups claim. This, of course, is not to argue that it is good for children to be involved in war or that war itself is either necessary or desirable. But it does attempt to answer the question of whether the current involvement of children in combat reflects a substantive historical shift in the role of children in warfare. The second question is to try to understand the factors that draw children into armed conflicts. This is an attempt to flesh out mass-media and human-rights reports that ignore, and indeed systematically sidestep, the role of children as activists, agents and decision makers in situations of extraordinary danger and stress.

To help answer these questions, I have closely examined three situations involving child soldiers. The first is the case of Sierra Leone where, as illustrated above, the use of child soldiers on all sides of the civil war has served as a bleak and horrific reminder of the exploitation of children as well as of the capacity of young children to engage in atrocious acts of violence.

The second case is the *intifada* in Israel and Palestine where the role of children in the Palestinian uprising has been both vilified and lionized. Israeli and Palestinian children have been killed in the conflict, but young Palestinians in particular have actively participated in civil protests as well as armed and unarmed attacks upon Israeli soldiers and civilians. Palestinian children have been labeled alternatively either as heroic martyrs or dupes of adult politics. Moreover, the Israeli-Palestinian conflict also brings to light the difficulties human-rights groups have in immunizing themselves from judgments rooted in politics.

The third case is Jewish youth resistance to the Nazis in World War II, both in the Warsaw Ghetto and in partisan groups in eastern Poland. Here the participation of children in armed conflict is usually regarded as nothing short of heroic. Jewish children and youth who were members of Zionist and socialist youth groups formed the core of armed resistance, and many young Jews fleeing for their lives found safety through their absorption into partisan units operating in the forests of Eastern Europe.

These cases put forward a major challenge to humanitarian ideas and to international law. In each instance, children appear as vital social and political actors who shape the dynamics of violence and conflict. In each, the actual actions and behaviors of children subvert idealized concepts of vulnerability and innocence contained in human-rights discourse.

Children in Combat Is a Serious Issue

I want to stress that even with this recognition, the point remains that the issue of children in combat needs to be taken seriously. The Coalition to Stop the Use of Child Soldiers' *Global Report 2001* claims that worldwide some 300,000 children are fighting as soldiers with government armed forces and armed oppositions. Hundreds of thousands more have been recruited into paramilitaries, civil militias and a wide variety of non-state armed groups.

There is now under way a major humanitarian effort to end the participation of children in armed conflict. This effort is led by various agencies of the United Nations, the International Committee of the Red Cross and the Coalition to Stop the Use of Child Soldiers. These groups have joined together to promote an international ban on the military recruitment and use of children as soldiers. These organizations, both individually and collectively, have been responsible for those provisions of the Rome Statute of the International Criminal Court that define the recruitment and use of child soldiers as a war crime.

Despite the seriousness of the issue, the current child-soldier crisis does not constitute a radical change in the way in which young people are drawn into warfare. Instead, the child-soldier crisis is a product of the globalization of new ideas about warfare and human rights. It arises out of the convergence of three powerful trends: first, the globalization of Western concepts of childhood; second, the

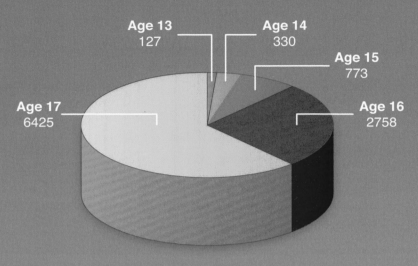

Number of Soldiers Under 18 Years of Age During the American Civil War

Age 13 127

Age 14 330

Age 15 773

Age 16 2758

Age 17 6425

Taken from: Benjamin A. Gould, *Investigations in the Military and Anthropological Statistics of American Soldiers.* New York: Herd & Houghton, 1869.

long-standing effort to criminalize all warfare; and third, the desire of nation-states, especially but not exclusively weak nation-states, to redefine rebellion, insurgency and separatism as criminal and to draw the world community into the suppression of rebellion. The union of these trends has created the problem of the "child soldier."

But the reasons for children fighting have not changed significantly. Sometimes they fight to save their lives, and at other times they fight for honor, glory or revenge. In some instances, they fight because they have been forcibly conscripted and even kidnapped (and horribly abused). In other words, they mostly fight for the same reasons adults do.

Children have Historically Been involved in Battle

The young have always been on or near the field of battle. In preindustrial societies what we know of young people in combat shows that there is no single fixed chronological age at which young people enter into the actions, dramas and rituals of war. Anthropologists have had frequent encounters with children at war. Among the Dinka of the Sudan, boys were initiated into adulthood at an age between 16 and 18 and immediately received gifts of well-designed spears that symbolized the military function of youth.

Among Native Americans of the plains such as the 19th-century Cheyenne, boys joined their first war parties when they were about 14 to 15 years old and slowly developed into seasoned warriors. Sometimes, as in many of the societies of East Africa such as the Maasai and Samburu, adolescent boys of varying chronological ages were collectively inducted into the status of warriors. Elsewhere, even among the Yanamano of Venezuela and Brazil, for whom warfare was especially valorized, adolescents largely set their own pace in determining when they wanted to take up the adult role of warrior.

There is no single rule for determining when the young are fit to be warriors. It depends on a wide variety of practical issues, since young men would have to be in a position to personally demonstrate their physical and emotional fitness for these roles. There is clear evidence that in some societies young people are deliberately socialized into highly aggressive behavior, and both individual and collective violence is highly esteemed, whereas in others more emphasis is based upon the peaceful resolution of disputes. The overall picture suggests that chronological boundaries between childhood and adulthood are highly varied and rooted in the historical experience of each society and culture.

Until recently, child soldiers in Western Europe and the United States were called "boy soldiers." Since the Middle Ages boy soldiers were routinely recruited into the British military, and by the late 19th century various institutions emerged that organized and systematized their recruitment. In Great Britain, the Royal Hibernium Military School was founded in 1765 for the children of so called "rank-and-file soldiers." It had its origins as an orphanage for working class and poor boys and quickly established links to the military. Among the earliest recruits were

12- and 13-year-olds, who were placed in regiments and served under Gen. [Thomas] Gage to suppress the growing American Revolution in 1774.

Children Fought in the Revolutionary and Civil Wars

A wide variety of data also supports the presence of the very young on the American side of the Revolutionary War. Until the 20th century most military service in the West was voluntary; but even with the emergence of conscription, the recruitment of child soldiers continued as schools and military apprenticeship programs directed boys into the military.

Throughout the Civil War, youngsters followed brothers, fathers and even teachers into battle. They often had support roles but quickly graduated into combat roles. They were sometimes recruited at school and, when necessary, used weapons that were cut down and adapted for use by smaller people. David Baily Freemen, "Little Dave," enlisted in the Confederate army at age 11, first accompanying his older brother as an aide-de-camp and then as a "marker" for a survey team before finally fighting against [General William] Sherman's army. Joseph John Clem (who changed his name to John Lincoln Clem) officially enlisted in the Union army at age 10 although he had been a camp follower since age 9. Gilbert "Little Gib" Van Zandt, age 10, followed his teacher into the Ohio Volunteer Infantry where he joined his father, uncles and friends. He joined up when recruiters arrived at his school despite his mother's pleas that he was "too young to fight." Clarence D. McKenzie, a drummer boy for Brooklyn's 13th Regiment was killed at Annapolis, Md., when he was only 12. His funeral, held on July 14, 1861, was attended by 3,000 people. A statue of the boy and his drum was erected to commemorate his sacrifice and is still one of the most visited graves in Brooklyn's Greenwood cemetery today.

The actual number of boy soldiers in the Civil War is uncertain. Although there have been exaggerations, careful historical analysis suggests that between 250,000 and 420,000 boy soldiers, including many in their early teens to even younger, served in the Union and Confederate armies. On the whole, between 10 and 20 percent of recruits were under 18. Applying modern humanitarian terminology, the war to end slavery was in large part fought by child soldiers in numbers even greater than those found in contemporary wars.

The Coalition to Stop the Use of Child Soldiers launched its global report on child soldiers by recounting Ismael Baeh's harrowing story about being a child soldier in Sierra Leone.

How Child Soldiers Were Understood

But numbers alone do not tell the whole story. Of equal importance is how the participation of boy soldiers in war was understood. Writings about boy soldiers in the aftermath of the Civil War celebrate the nobility and sacrifice of young boys in battle. The existence of developmental differences between boys and men were recognized but understood rather differently from today. Although young boys were regarded as impulsive and less mature than older men, this quality was recast as grand and heroic. Testimonials collected after the Civil War describe boy soldiers as enduring battle with "patience and gaiety" and those who died as having "made their peace with God."

Equally important, the experience of battle, however horrific, was not understood as destroying the lives of children but ennobling them. Boy soldiers who survived intact were deemed respected citizens whose contribution to civic life was enhanced by the experience of war.

These historical examples put forward radically different views of children in battle than contained in contemporary humanitarian accounts focusing purely on abusive recruitment of children by force. They indicate that child soldiers are not a new phenomenon, and that child soldiers are not always victims. Rather, for many, child soldiers serving their country or cause has been considered honorable. The issue is not simple. Atrocities have occurred which cannot be ignored. Yet, we still need to recognize that children, even young children—when faced with desperate situations and injustice—can be smart and heroic, and act independent of adult authority and power.

What You Should Know About Child Labor

Defining Child Labor

In a 2007 series of reports, World Vision International states:

- For the purposes of this publication, "child means every human being below the age of eighteen years unless under the law applicable to the child, majority is attained earlier."

According to International Labour Organization, the worst forms of child labor are:

- all forms of slavery or practices similar to slavery, such as the sale and trafficking of children, debt bondage and serfdom and forced or compulsory labor, including forced or compulsory recruitment of children for use in armed conflict;
- the use, procuring, or offering of a child for prostitution, for the production of pornography, or for pornographic performances;
- the use, procuring, or offering of a child for illicit activities, in particular for the production and trafficking of drugs, as defined in the relevant international treaties;
- work which, by its nature or the circumstances in which it is carried out, is likely to harm the health, safety, or morals of children.

World Vision International describes these characteristics of child labor:

- Children start working at an earlier age in rural areas rather than in cities.

- Eighty percent of children work in an informal economy.
- Work prevents children from attending school or limits their academic performance.
- Ninety percent of child workers between the ages of ten and fourteen, earn wages that are equal to or below the minimum wage, approximately 20 percent lower than the income of an adult with a seventh-grade education level. Some children are paid an even lower salary than that or are paid in kind.
- Children do not have labor rights.

According to Free the Children, the following are some of the causes of child labor:
- Poverty—poor families need to keep as many family members working as possible to ensure income security and survival.
- Inadequate school facilities—many children live in areas that do not have adequate school facilities, so they work. Many countries do not have free compulsory education for all, which creates an obstacle to sending working children to school.
- Family size—poor households tend to have more children, and in large families there is a greater likelihood that children will work and have lower school attendance and completion.
- Immoral employers—some employers hire children because they can pay them less; they also offer poor working conditions because children are less likely to complain.

World Vision International describes these consequences of child labor:
- Social and Moral
  - Encourages inequality
  - Violates the fundamental human rights of children and adolescents
  - Leads to a loss of self-esteem, problems of social adaptation, and trauma

- Physical and Psychological
  - Chronic diseases
  - Dependence on medicines
  - Physical and psychological abuse

- Economic
  - Working children fall behind in school by an average of two grades or two school years in the long run, which means a salary that is 20 percent lower during their adult lives.
  - Loss of buying power in the national market.

Regarding the Current World Situation

Stop Child Labor reports that
- there are 218 million child laborers in the world;
- 14 percent of all children between five and seventeen years old are child laborers;
- one out of seven children around the world is a child laborer;
- 63 percent of children in Mali, 38 percent in Cambodia, and 47 percent in Burkina Faso are child laborers;
- 22 percent of child laborers work in the service industry—retail, restaurants and hotels, transportation, finance, business, community and social services;
- 9 percent of child laborers work in industry—mining, quarrying, manufacturing, construction, and public utilities;
- 69 percent of child laborers work in agriculture—farming, hunting, fishing, and forestry;
- every year twenty-two thousand children die in work-related accidents;
- the number of child laborers fell 11 percent globally from 2002 to 2006, and the number of children in hazardous work decreased 26 percent.

UNICEF reports that:
- in the eastern and southern Africa region (ESAR), 36 percent of children aged five to fourteen are engaged in some form of labor, compared with 13 percent in South Asia and 16 percent in developing countries (excluding China)—the highest rate of all regions;
- the ESAR regional average, however, masks a wide variation in national rates of child labor, ranging from 9 percent in Swaziland to 53 percent in Ethiopia;

- boys are more likely to be engaged in child labor than are girls, although those working in households are overwhelmingly girls;
- sexual exploitation is recognized as one of the most hazardous forms of child labor;
- studies show that girls are more often abused and exploited, although boys are also affected;
- commercial sexual exploitation is a particular concern in a number of countries in ESAR, including Kenya, South Africa, and Madagascar;
- in Uganda, an increased number of children have been withdrawn from exploitation and hazardous labor through the provision of alternatives, including support to return to their communities of origin;
- Angola has developed a code of conduct under the coordination of the Ministry of Tourism aimed at increasing protection against sexual exploitation and abuse, especially during the Africa Cup of Nations football tournament in January 2010;
- Mozambique introduced police victim support centres, which in 2009 assisted more than fourteen thousand children and women who survived acts of violence, abuse, and exploitation.

Changes in Recent Years

The International Labour Organization's *Facts on Child Labor 2010* reports that:
- child labor continues to decline, but only modestly—a 3 percent reduction in the four-year period covered by the new estimates (2004–2008). In the previous report (covering the period 2000–2004), there had been a 10 percent decrease;
- among five- to fourteen-year-olds, the number of child laborers has declined by 10 percent and the number of children in hazardous work by 31 percent;
- while the number of children in hazardous work, often used as a proxy for the worst forms of child labor, is declining, the overall rate of reduction has slowed, though there are still 115 million children in hazardous work;

- the number of girls in child labor has decreased by 15 percent while the number of girls in hazardous work has decreased by 24 percent; boys, however, saw their work increase, both in terms of incidence rates and in absolute numbers while the extent of hazardous work among boys remained relatively stable;
- there has been a 20 percent increase in child labor in the fifteen- to seventeen-year-old age group—from 52 million to 62 million;
- most child laborers continue to work in agriculture (60 percent), and only one in five working children is in paid employment, while the overwhelming majority are unpaid family workers.

What You Should Do About Child Labor

Gather Information

The first step in grappling with any complex and controversial issue is to be informed about it. Gather as much information as you can from a variety of sources. The essays in this book form an excellent starting point, representing a variety of viewpoints and approaches to the topic. Your school or local library will be another source of useful information; look there for relevant books, magazines, and encyclopedia entries. The bibliography and organizations to contact sections of this book will give you useful starting points in gathering additional information. There are numerous organizations worldwide that defend the rights of child laborers, some by working to eliminate child labor and others by defending the rights of children who do work. Visit the websites of the organizations listed in the organizations to contact section to learn more. Do an Internet search for "child labor" to find additional organizations.

Identify the Issues Involved

Once you have gathered your information, review it methodically to discover the key issues involved. Notice that many organizations use slogans such as "stop child labor" or "end child labor now." The issue appears to be clear cut—child labor should be stopped in all forms, in all places; however, as you begin to study the issue you will realize that the issue is not that simple. Think about questions like these: Why is child labor an issue? What harm can come to children who work? What can children gain by working? Is it right for children to work in some forms of labor but not in others? How does the age of a child affect the labor they can or should do? Is child labor more acceptable in some parts of the world than in others? Should it be? What other questions occur to you as you learn more about the issue?

Evaluate Your Information Sources

As you learn about a topic, make sure to evaluate the sources of the information you have discovered. Authors always speak from their own perspective, which influences the way they perceive a subject and how they present information.

Consider the authors' experience and backgrounds. Have they observed child labor firsthand or experienced it themselves? Or do they speak from material they have read and statistics that have been gathered by others? Someone with a personal perspective has a very different point of view from someone who has studied the issue at a distance. Both can be useful, but it is important to recognize what the author bases his or her opinion on. For example, someone who has worked on a farm as a child may look at his or her own experience as a positive growth opportunity and report that children should be allowed to work on farms without strict limits. Someone else could report from an academic research perspective that other children studied did not have the same positive experiences working on farms and that, therefore, child labor on farms should be regulated. Both points of view are valid. They just present different perspectives.

Examine Your Own Perspective

Consider your own beliefs, feelings, and biases on this issue. Before you began studying, did you have an opinion about child labor? If so, what influenced you to have this opinion—friends, family, personal experience, something you read or heard in the media? Be careful to acknowledge your own viewpoint, and be willing to learn about other sides of the issue. Make sure to study and honestly consider opinions that are different from yours. Do they make some points that might convince you to change your mind? Do they raise more questions that you need to think about? Or does looking at other viewpoints more solidly convince you of your own initial perspective?

Form Your Own Opinion

Once you have gathered and organized information, identified the issues involved, and examined your own perspective, you will be ready to form an opinion on child labor and to advocate for that position in debates and discussions. You may decide that child labor worldwide must be stopped. Or you may decide that children should be allowed to work but also be required to attend school. Or you could decide that children should work as many hours as they want and not worry about getting a formal education. These are just a few of the opinions that you might form after learning about this issue. Whatever position you take, be prepared to explain it clearly based on facts, evidence, and well-thought-out beliefs.

Take Action

Once you have developed your position on child labor, you can consider turning your beliefs into action. Advocating your position in discussions and debates is one place to start. You also might want to join an organization that shares your beliefs about child labor—check out the organizations to contact section of this book for some starting points. These organizations offer ways that you can support working children or advocate for change in conditions and regulations regarding working children. If you would like to contact your political representatives directly to express your position on child labor and what you think should be done about it, the website www.usa.gov/Contact/Elected.shtml can help you get started.

You may decide that you are particularly interested in working conditions of children in the United States or in your own community. The United States Department of Labor sponsors a website called "Youth Rules!" at www.youthrules.dol.gov that helps teens, parents, and employers know about the current rules and regulations regarding child labor. The site includes a section on how you can help make sure that employers comply with these laws.

ORGANIZATIONS TO CONTACT

The editors have compiled the following list of organizations concerned with the issues debated in this book. The descriptions are derived from materials provided by the organizations. All have publications or information available for interested readers. The list was compiled on the date of publication of the present volume; the information provided here may change. Be aware that many organizations take several weeks or longer to respond to inquiries, so allow as much time as possible for the receipt of requested materials.

Anti-Slavery International
Thomas Clarkson House, The Stableyard
Broomgrove Rd., London SW9 9TL United Kingdom
+44 (0)20 7501 8920 • fax: +44 (0)20 7738 4110
e-mail: info@antislavery.org
website: http://antislavery.org/english

Anti-Slavery International, founded in 1839, is the world's oldest international human rights organization. Anti-Slavery International works at local, national, and international levels to eliminate all forms of slavery around the world. Their work includes campaigns against child labor and human trafficking. The organization publishes its research and produces its own resources for public education on contemporary and historical slavery.

Butterflies
U-4, Green Park Extension, New Delhi 110 016, India
+91 11 2616 3935 or +91 11 2619 1063
fax: +91 11 2619 6117 • e-mail: butterflies@vsnl.com
website: www.butterflieschildrights.org

Butterflies is a registered voluntary organization working with street and working children in Delhi, India, since 1989. Butterflies believes in the right of every child, including street and working children, to have a full-fledged childhood where she/he has the right to protection, respect, opportunities, and participation in his/her growth and development. The organization's main aim is to empower street and working children with skills and knowledge to protect their rights and to develop them as respected and productive citizens. The website includes links to the organization's newsletter and the latest edition of *National Children's Times* and *Delhi Children's Times*.

The Child Labor Coalition
National Consumers' League, 1701 K St. NW, Ste. 1200, Washington, DC 20006
e-mail: reidm@nclnet.org• website: http://clc.designannexe.com

The Child Labor Coalition is a national network for the exchange of information about child labor. It provides a forum and a unified voice on protecting working minors and ending child labor exploitation and provides informational and educational outreach sectors to combat child labor abuses and promote progressive initiatives and legislation. An online media library includes videos, photographs, documents, and maps related to child labor.

Child Rights Information Network (CRIN)
East Studio 2, Pontypool Pl., London SE1 8QF, United Kingdom
+44 (0)20 7401 2257 • e-mail: info@crin.org
website: http://crin.org

CRIN is a global network coordinating and promoting information and action on child rights. CRIN presses for rights, not charity, for children and is guided by a passion for putting children's rights at the top of the global agenda by addressing root causes and promoting systematic change. It has a variety of publications on child abuse and child labor available for download from its website.

The Coalition to Stop the Use of Child Soldiers
International Secretariat, 4th Fl., 9 Marshalsea Rd., London SE1 1EP United Kingdom

+44 (0)20 7367 4110 • fax: +44 (0)20 7367 4129
e-mail: info@child-soldiers.org • website: www.child-soldiers.org

The Coalition to Stop the Use of Child Soldiers is an international organization whose purpose is to prevent the recruitment and use of children as soldiers; to secure their demobilization; and to promote their rehabilitation and reintegration into society. It accomplishes these goals through advocacy, research, and monitoring. The coalition's goal is to promote the adoption and adherence to national, regional, and international legal standards prohibiting the military recruitment and use in hostilities of any person younger than eighteen years of age and the recognition and enforcement of this standard by all armed groups, both governmental and nongovernmental. The coalition's website provides reports, news, photos, and a bibliography of books and materials about child soldiers.

The Concerned for Working Children (CWC)
303/2, L B Shastri Nagar Vimanapura Post
Bangalore 560 017, Karnataka, India
+91 80 2523 4611 • fax: +91 80 2523 5034
e-mail: cwc@pobox.com • website: www.workingchild.org

The Concerned for Working Children has been working in the field of child labor in India since 1980. CWC works with local governments, community, and working children themselves to implement viable, comprehensive, sustainable, and appropriate solutions in partnership with all the major actors so that children do not have to work. It empowers working children so that they may be their own first line of defense and participate in an informed manner in all decisions concerning themselves. Its website includes various tools for additional research.

Fisek Institute Science and Action Foundation for Child Labour
Selanik Cad. 52/4 Kizilay, Ankara, Turkey
+90 312 419 7811 • fax: +90 312 425 2801
website: www.fisek.org

The Fisek Institute is a nongovernmental organization acting in the field of occupational health and safety at the national level. It aims to raise the consciousness of the public in order to remove the reasons forcing children to work; to eliminate the factors that are dangerous for their health and safety at work; and to ensure improvement of health, identity, and self-esteem of the working children. Research, essays, and maps are available on its website.

Free the Children International
233 Carlton St., Toronto, ON M5A 2L2 Canada
(416) 925-5894 • fax: (416) 925-8242

Free the Children (USA)
PO Box 32099, Hartford, CT 06150-2099
(800) 203-9091 (USA only) •e-mail: info@freethechildren.com
website: www.freethechildren.com

Free the Children is a worldwide network of children helping children through education, with more than a million youth involved in its education and development programs in forty-five countries. Founded in 1995 by international child rights activist Craig Kielburger (a child himself at the time), the primary goals of the organization are to free children from poverty and exploitation and to free young people from the notion that they are powerless to bring about positive change in the world. Through domestic empowerment programs and leadership training, Free the Children inspires young people to develop themselves as socially conscious global citizens and to become agents of change for their peers around the world. Brochures and reports are available for download at the Free the Children website.

Free the Slaves
1320 Nineteenth St. NW, Ste. 600, Washington, DC 20036
(202) 775-7480 • e-mail: info@freetheslaves.net
website: www.freetheslaves.net

Free the Slaves is a not-for-profit organization founded in 2000 in response to Dr. Kevin Bales's book *Disposable People*. The organization is made up of people who do not want to live in a world with slavery, which is defined as forced work without pay under threat of violence and without the ability to leave. Free the Slaves liberates slaves of all ages around the world, helps them rebuild their lives, and researches real-world solutions to eradicate slavery forever. The organization uses world-class research and compelling stories from the frontlines of slavery to convince the powerful and the powerless that slavery can be ended.

Global March Against Child Labor Foundation
L-6, Kalkaji, New Delhi 110 019, India
+91 11 4132 9025 • fax: +91 11 4053 2072
e-mail: info@globalmarch.org • website: www.globalmarch.org

The Global March Against Child Labor is a worldwide movement to protect and promote the rights of all children. The organization is especially concerned with children's right to receive a free, meaningful education and to be free from economic exploitation and from performing any work that is likely to be harmful to the child's physical, mental, spiritual, moral, or social development. Its publications include reviews of child labor in countries such as Costa Rica, Bangladesh, Chile, and Niger and are available for download from its website.

Human Rights Watch
350 Fifth Ave., 34th Fl., New York, NY 10118-3299
(212) 290-4700 • fax: (212) 736-1300
website: www.hrw.org

Human Rights Watch is an independent nongovernmental organization dedicated to protecting the human rights of people around the world. Human Rights Watch investigates and exposes human rights violations and holds abusers accountable, challenges governments and those who hold power to end abusive practices and respect international human rights law, and enlists the public and the international community to support the cause of human rights for all. Human Rights watch publishes numerous studies on bonded child labor, child soldiers, child domestic workers, and child slaves that are available on its website.

International Center on Child Labor and Education (ICCLE)

888 Sixteenth St. NW, Ste. 400, Washington, DC 20006
(202) 974-8124 • fax: (202) 974-8123
e-mail: sjoshi@iccle.org • website: www.iccle.org

ICCLE is a nonprofit organization dedicated to mobilizing worldwide efforts to advance the rights of all children, especially the rights to receive a free and meaningful education and to be free from economic exploitation and any work that is hazardous, interferes with a child's education, or is harmful to a child's health or physical, mental, spiritual, moral, or social development. The center serves as the international advocacy office of the Global March Against Child Labor, a movement representing some two thousand organizations in 140 countries intended to highlight child slavery and hazardous child labor. The website has publications available for download on global child labor, including child labor in South America, Africa, Asia, and elsewhere.

International Cocoa Initiative

28 rue du Village, CH-1214, Vernier/Genève, Switzerland
+41 (0)22 341 4725 • e-mail: info@cocoainitiative.org
website: www.cocoainitiative.org

The International Cocoa Initiative is a partnership of concerned companies in the cocoa industry, labor unions, government, and nongovernmental organizations that seeks to eliminate child labor and forced labor in the cocoa production industry. The organization also seeks to stimulate local communities to share their concerns and help them develop their own plans to address issues such as education provision for the poor and better cocoa farming in order to support the changes in practices that will over time eliminate child labor in the sector. It also works to encourage local authorities to meet the expressed needs of the communities, support the development of national programs, and aim to inform the international debate. Resources available on its website include reports and statistics on child labor and forced labor in the cocoa industry.

International Initiative on Exploitative Child Labor (IIECL)

1016 S. Wayne St., Ste. 702, Arlington, VA 22204
(703) 920-0435 • e-mail: iiecl@endchildlabor.org
website: www.endchildlabor.org

The IIECL, also commonly known as the International Initiative to End Child Labor, is a US-based not-for-profit organization founded in 1998 that conducts and/or provides education, training, technical assistance, capacity building, research, social accountability auditing, resources, and evaluation services to public and private institutions and agencies, nongovernmental organizations, and international programmatic institutions that seek to eliminate the worst forms of child labor in the United States and around the world. Photos, videos, and publications are available on the organization's website.

The International Labour Organization (ILO)

4 route des Morillons, CH-1211, Genève 22, Switzerland
+41 (0)22 799 6111 • fax: +41 (0)22 798 8685
e-mail: ilo@ilo.org • website: www.ilo.org

The International Labour Organization is a United Nations agency responsible for drawing up and overseeing international labor standards. It is the only "tripartite" United Nations agency that brings together representatives of governments, employers, and workers to jointly shape policies and programs promoting decent work for all. Its main aims are to promote rights at work, encourage decent employment opportunities, enhance social protection, and strengthen dialogue in handling work-related issues. The ILO publishes numerous publications about global labor and child labor, including the magazine *World of Work*. Many of these publications are available free from its website.

International Research on Working Children (IREWOC)

Hooglandse Kerkgracht 17-H, 2312 HS, Leiden, The Netherlands
+31 (0)71 5122883 • e-mail: info@irewoc.nl
website: www.irewoc.nl

IREWOC was founded in 1992 to generate more research on child labor. It is a professional organization that looks at the issue of child labor from the perspective of child rights and with a focus on the sociocultural and economic environment. IREWOC has a variety of child labor publications available for download from its website.

Save the Children International
5 Tudor City Place, New York, NY 10017
(212) 370-2461 • fax: (212) 490-3395
e-mail: info@save-children-alliance.org
website: www.savethechildren.net

Save the Children is a global nonprofit organization founded in 1919 by Eglantyne Jebb. Save the Children encourages its supporters to put pressure on decision makers and opinion formers to change policies and practices, locally and globally, to ensure that children's rights become reality. Save the Children's vision is a world in which every child has the right to survival, protection, development, and participation. Its mission is to inspire breakthroughs in the way the world treats children and to achieve immediate and lasting change in their lives. Save the Children campaigns for long-term change in addition to providing shorter-term support to improve children's lives.

UNICEF
3 United Nations Plaza, New York, NY 10017
(212) 326-7000 • fax: (212) 887-7465
e-mail: information@unicefusa.org
website: www.unicef.org

UNICEF is a United Nations organization created to advocate for the protection of children's rights, to help meet children's basic needs, and to expand children's opportunities to reach their full potential. UNICEF strives to establish children's rights as enduring ethical principles and international standards of behavior toward children. Together with the International Labour Organization and World Bank, UNICEF participates in an interagency research project, Understanding Children's Work, that provides extensive data and information on child labor. UNICEF offers numerous publications, including a yearly summary called "The State of the World's Children," which is available for download from its website.

United States Department of Labor
200 Constitution Ave. NW, Washington, DC 20210
(866) 4-USA-DOL (487-2365) • TTY: (877) 889-5627
e-mail: globalkids@dol.gov • website: www.dol.gov/

The United States Department of Labor fosters and promotes the welfare of the job seekers, wage earners, and retirees of the United States by improving their working conditions, advancing their opportunities for profitable employment, protecting their retirement and health-care benefits, helping employers find workers, strengthening free collective bargaining, and tracking changes in employment, prices, and other national economic measurements. In carrying out this mission, the department administers a variety of federal labor laws, including those that guarantee workers' rights to safe and healthy working conditions, a minimum hourly wage and overtime pay, freedom from employment discrimination, unemployment insurance, and other income support. Numerous publications about child labor and labor in general are available on the Department of Labor's website.

BIBLIOGRAPHY

Books

Kevin Bales, *The Slave Next Door: Human Trafficking and Slavery in America Today*. Berkeley and Los Angeles: University of California Press, 2009.

David B. Batstone, *Not for Sale: The Return of the Global Slave Trade— and How We Can Fight It*. New York: HarperSanFrancisco, 2007.

Rachel Burr, *Vietnam's Children in a Changing World*. New Brunswick, NJ: Rutgers University Press, 2006.

Marito Garcia and Jean Fares, eds., *Youth in Africa's Labor Market*. Washington, DC: World Bank, 2008.

Allen D. Hertzke, *Freeing God's Children: The Unlikely Alliance for Global Human Rights*. Lanham, MD: Rowman & Littlefield, 2004.

Wendy Herumin, *Child Labor Today: A Human Rights Issue*. Berkeley Heights, NJ: Enslow, 2008.

Hugh D. Hindman, ed., *The World of Child Labor: An Historical and Regional Survey*. Armonk, NY: M.E. Sharpe, 2009.

Rachel Lynette, *Craig Kielburger: Founder of Free the Children*. Detroit: KidHaven, 2008.

Thomas A. Offit, *Conquistadores de la Calle: Child Street Labor in Guatemala City*. Austin: University of Texas Press, 2008.

E. Benjamin Skinner, *A Crime So Monstrous: Face-to-Face with Modern-Day Slavery*. New York: Free Press, 2008.

Burns H. Weston, ed., *Child Labor and Human Rights: Making Children Matter*. Boulder, CO: Lynne Rienner, 2005.

Periodicals

Marten van den Berge, "Working Children's Movements in Peru," *International Research on Working Children*, May 2007.

Coalition to Stop the Use of Child Soldiers, "Child Soldiers: Global Report 2008," 2008.

Deborah Dunn, "Is It Fair to Eat Chocolate?," *Skipping Stones*, November–December 2008.

Hans van de Glind and Joost Kooijmans, "Modern-Day Child Slavery," *Children & Society*, May 2008.

Samuel Grumiau, "Let Parents Earn and Children Learn," FNV Mondiaal (Dutch labor organization), May 2010.

Human Rights Watch, "Fields of Peril: Child Labor in U.S. Agriculture," 2010.

Natasa Kovasevic, "Child Slavery: India's Self-Perpetuating Drama," *Harvard International Review*, Summer 2007.

Jeylan T. Mortimer, "The Benefits and Risks of Adolescent Employment," *Prevention Researcher*, April 2010.

Ranee Khooshie Lal Panjabi, "Sacrificial Lambs of Globalization: Child Labor in the Twenty-First Century," *Denver Journal of International Law & Policy*, Summer 2009.

Sadaf Qureshi, "Blood Chocolate: A Just Dessert?," *Humanist*, September–October 2008.

Sam Taylor and Sarah Crowe, "On World Day Against Child Labor, One Nepali Girl's Story of a Fresh Start," UNICEF, June 12, 2009. www.unicef.org.

Dana Thomas, "The Fake Trade: Wanted for Stealing Childhoods," *Harper's Bazaar*, January 2007.

Fatima M. Umar, "Street Hawking: Oppressing the Girl Child or Family Economic Supplement?," *Journal of Instructional Psychology*, June 2009.

World Vision International, "Bolivia: Children Who Work in Tin Mines," June 2007.

World Vision International, "Brazil: Children Who Work in the Markets," June 2007.

World Vision International, "Chile: Children Who Work in the Mountains," June 2007.

INDEX

PICTURE CREDITS

AP Images/Jacques Brinon, 91

AP Images/Jennifer Graylock, 57

AP Images/Lawrence Jackson, 31

AP Images/Hermann J. Knippertz, 7

AP Images/Donna McWilliam, 63

© blickwinkel/Alamy, 44

Colin Cuthbert/Photo Researchers, Inc., 10

Zoom Doss/AFP/Getty Images, 77

Romeo Gacad/AFP/Getty Images, 21

Gale/Cengage Learning, 12, 18, 28, 33, 38, 50, 54, 67, 70, 80, 88

Lowell George/National Geographic/Getty Images, 27

Nature's Images/Photo Researchers, Inc., 37

Jim Spellman/WireImage/Getty Images, 49

Eduardo Verdugo/AFP/Getty Images, 73